The Rainbow Connection

By Rebecca Clark

Cover designed by
Sue Jackson

All biblical quotations are from the Revised Standard
Version unless otherwise noted.

Contents

Preface

Precious Friends:

This is a book about *light, love, reality, the Christ Spirit, you, and the wonderful Rainbow Connection* between you and the creative source of all—God.

I love rainbows. The sight of those brilliant colors reaching across the sky ever touches an inner spark which prompts a remembrance of my rich inheritance as a child of God. What is a rainbow? Webster's Dictionary describes a rainbow as: *An arc of colors found opposite the sun by the refraction of the sun's rays in rain, spray, or mist.* Scripture says the rainbow is the token of the covenant between God and man. Charles Fillmore, in the *Metaphysical Bible Dictionary*, speaks of the rainbow as . . . *a sign in the heavens symbolizing the perfect blending of the race into obedience to one harmonious Christ principle—the endless circle of natural perfection coming out of obedience to divine law.* I perceive the rainbow as a spiritual catapult, a reminder of our oneness with God and with all people, and the cosmic prism through which the light of increasing understanding can shine.

There are two kinds of light with which a child of God can glean understanding of the earth plane, and it seems that the light energy being used by most brings *intellectual* understanding. The other light, the Christ light, brings the true *spiritual* understanding to all who have the faith to seek greater attunement with God through prayer and meditation. Every thought of prayer, every exercise of human willpower in a constructive expression, aligned with the divine will of God, adds to the creative restorative power of peace on Earth and good will toward all.

The objective of the various true spiritual activities unfolding through the ages has been that of assisting the sincere individual who is searching for Truth to find God within his own heart and mind, not in some far-off vista of blue sky and mythological expression. Adepts and their students have attempted to assist each seeker in finding the God-spark of the creative source *alive* within themselves.

Then, once having recognized the Source, each person can allow it the privilege, honor, and courtesy of directing the lifestream so that the divine plan—that of reaching Christ consciousness—might be fulfilled. The God plan is the divine plan which brings an expanding awareness of blessings, happiness, eternal life, and light to all.

Conditions on Earth today are vastly different from those even fifty years ago. Thus, the needs of the human family are different from those of ages past. We live in a time of tremendous change. We think and feel in progressive capacities as we have evolved from the ox cart, through the horse and buggy, the automobile, the airplane, supersonic jets, and into the age of space travel; from a pale tallow candle to lamps, gas, electricity, and quantum advances into the age of electronics. The children of today live with, understand, and use items that even the greatest minds of the past knew nothing about! The reality of life is that one cannot live in the past or in the future. You can actually live only in the eternal Now. And right Now can be the time your dreams come true. Whether they do or not depends upon *your faith* and *your constructive actions.* If you and I were mere human beings, perhaps it might be foolish to believe our dreams could become manifest. But we are *spiritual beings* endowed with the very power of God to help us achieve our great and good desires! We are not puppets on a string!

Through the Spirit, soul, and body of each person flows the unlimited power of the universe with which to achieve all good. The creative Source expects each one to use this spiritual dominion. How else does growth unfold? How else are achievements accomplished? How else can we progress? Through what other measures can we contribute to the good of all mankind!

In Truth, you are a glorious child of God, a being of light! You are filled with a radiance that cannot be dimmed by lack, limitation, or so-called misfortune. Although circumstances may seem to proclaim dark clouds and storms, there is always within you the clear, unfailing, redeeming, restoring light of Truth, and the promises of the rainbow!

Become still within your thoughts and feelings for a moment. Declare for yourself: *I am the light of the world.* Stay relaxed in mind and body until you become immersed in light in thought and feeling, until you recognize an upliftment and regeneration in your entire being of Spirit, soul, and body. Now, expand your consciousness in a "Rainbow Meditation."

A Rainbow Meditation

The living light of God is the Truth of my
soul.
The presence of the Christ Spirit guides
every sure step on my journey of life.
Yes, the Christ—the presence of light,
peace, joy, love, life, and substance—is
ever within, about, before, and beside
me.
I am divine Spirit. I am a child of God.
In God I live and move and have my being.
Where there is light, there can be no
darkness.
I daily look to the light of Truth and radiate
the prismatic colors of my soul. As the
rainbow hues of red, orange, yellow,
green, blue, violet, and indigo pour
their vibratory essence into my daily
world, I hold the thought that whatever I do this day and every day, I do
in light.
Although clouds may appear on the horizon

of my world, never for one moment does the promise of God's presence grow dim or fade.

It shines freely, clearly, steadily, and brightly. Permanently!

I now mentally step into a blazing sphere of brilliant golden light.

I acknowledge the light.

I live in the light.

I work in the light.

I play in the light.

I am lovingly enfolded in the light.

The living, loving light of God is with me always.

I am grateful and joyfully give thanks for the light, and go forth now to do all that needs to be done by me.

And so it is!

Rebecca Clark

The Rainbow Connection

Rainbow Promises for Your Spiritual Needs

...our inner nature is being renewed every day. (II Cor. 4:16)

"I came that they may have life, and have it abundantly." (John 10:10)

...he who does what is true comes to the light, that it may be clearly seen that his deeds have been wrought in God. (John 3:21)

"Awake, O sleeper, and arise from the dead, and Christ shall give you light." (Eph. 5:14)

"...All things are possible to him who believes...." (Mark 9:23)

He who walks in integrity will be delivered... (Prov. 28:18)

"...I will restore health to you, and your wounds I will heal..." (Jer. 30:17)

"And whatever you ask in prayer, you will receive, if you have faith." (Matt. 21:22)

... now you are light in the Lord; walk as children of light ... (Eph. 5:8)

... he will give his angels charge of you to guard you in all your ways. (Psalms 91:11)

... he who listens to me will dwell secure and will be at ease ... (Prov. 1:33)

The Original Rainbow Story

*T*hroughout our planetary home there are people in every nation who feel an increase of love for humanity, people who seek to bring peace, understanding, and brotherhood into the world in which we live. It matters not what creed or dogma these people follow, or what faith they claim. The sincere prayers of all people seeking greater light unite as a part of the great good for the world. As seekers of the light, we are joined in the invisible bond of God's eternal love for all humanity. We have faith in humankind. We know that good and the light are victorious over all seeming negativities. We seek ways to bring freedom, justice, and peace into the lives of people the world over.

The light of the Christ means to us what the light of the sun means to the Earth. The seed of our divinity starts to germinate and grow into a beautiful expression as the light of the Christ nature stirs within us. Our spiritual radiance turns darkness into light. It transforms a barren life into one of abundance and productivity.

Earth's nature is light. Our nature is light. Light is within us and all about us. Have you ever thought of yourself as a child of light? It's true! You are! Jesus constantly identified Himself with light, for He realized that He came into the world as a radiant son of light. He said: *"I am the light of the world; he who follows me will not walk in darkness, but will have the light of life."* (Jn. 8:12) Jesus brought us into the picture when He said: *"You are the light of the world. . . . let your light so shine before men, that they may see your good works and give glory to your father who is in heaven."* (Matt. 5:14, 16)

As the light of understanding dawns upon us, we become quickened and warmed by the inner stirring of divine Love. Our response to this spiritual urge is to more fully express the realities of Truth in daily living.

Mac Dossoir in "Aesthetics and Theory of Act" (1906) states: *Only the very beginnings of a word's life are like a glimpse of sunlight. Then the word is still fresh and vigorous, not faded or worn out, like the words "faith" and "will" have become. These words have be-*

4

come degenerated in popular usage; but if one can go back to their pure, original meanings, faith and will sparkle like diamonds.

That *glimpse of sunlight* was one of the aims of Charles Fillmore, cofounder of Unity. Mr. Fillmore cherished the idea that what was really important was the message for the ages contained in the books of the Bible. He was an innovative thinker, a pioneer in metaphysical thought, and he reserved the right to change his mind as greater understanding of universal principles unfolded for him. Mr. Fillmore realized that everything comes by consent. We get what we really and truly want and consent to.

As we begin to understand that the stories in Scripture are the life stories of each of us, we learn ways and means of taking charge in our lives and becoming masters over situations and circumstances.

There is something greater within each of us than the "me," or my current understanding. Often, we give too much credit or place too much blame on one particular level of our being—the current level of our conscious know-how. This is the part of us referred to in Truth teachings as the small "s" self. This part of us is incapable of many things which that part of us that is greater than self accomplishes quite well when necessary. We recognize this greater-than-self part of us as the Christ within, the I AM of us, the Lord of our being.

Noah's Story

It was the Christ self of Noah that heard the voice of God speaking and obeyed.

Scripture tells us Noah was a just and God-loving man who lived in a period when the *... earth was corrupt ... filled with violence.* (Gen. 6:11) God told Noah that all living creatures would be destroyed with a great flood. Noah was instructed to build a wooden Ark with three decks and to stock it with every kind of food.

Before the flood, Noah entered the Ark with his wife, his three sons—Shem, Ham, and Japheth—and their wives, and a male and female of each living creature.

It then rained for forty days and nights, and floodwaters rose until the mountaintops were covered. The Ark with its strange cargo floated on the water's surface while all other life on Earth perished.

After five months, the floodwater began to

recede, and in the seventh month the Ark came to rest on top of Mount Ararat. Noah waited several more months while the waters subsided then sent out a raven and a dove which did not find land. A week later the dove went forth and returned with an olive leaf in its beak. The third time out of the Ark, the dove did not return, indicating the emergence of land. A year after entering, Noah and his family and all the living creatures emerged from the Ark.

Now, realizing that Noah's story is also the story of you and me and every person, what is the understanding presented?

Scripture tells us that *Noah found favor in the eyes of the Lord.* (Gen. 6:8) Metaphysically, the word Noah means calm, rest, equilibrium; and he and his family are factors within us which enable us to remain calm, poised, and balanced regardless of seeming appearances. When we are at peace with our indwelling Lord, we are protected. Even when we are most unreasonable, most negative, most boring, there is always a private reserve of us that is understanding, positive, and informative. There is that part of us which is always at rest even when some other part is banging heads with bricks! Noah! It is this part of us which is inviolate, untouched, which is preserved and strengthened for us as we adventure through the disciplines and purifications of life's educational experiences.

When the great flood came, not all was destroyed. Charles Fillmore says: *The ark represents a positive, saving state of consciousness, which agrees with or forms a covenant with the principle of Being . . .* "

It is important to realize that all that is within us of a true and constructive nature does not have to be dissolved and reformed. It simply transforms itself to greater expression right where it is.

Yes, the unexpected changes and upheavals in the outer affairs of our lives, or strange senses in the physical body, or unexplainable moods in the feeling nature, are symptomatic of times of experiencing this "inner flood" process. It is a partial externalizing of the breaking up or dissolving of congestion and crystallization which is often called chemicalization. And we will go into this activity in a later chapter.

The Flood Is Over

When the waters receded, Noah built an

altar and gave offering to God. Then came an eternal promise of God:

"I will never again curse the ground because of man, for the imagination of man's heart is evil from his youth; neither will I ever again destroy every living creature as I have done." (Gen. 8:21)

A little later God continued:

"Behold, I establish my covenant with you and your descendants after you, and with every living creature that is with you . . . as many as came out of the ark. I establish my covenant with you, that never again shall all flesh be cut off by the waters of a flood, and never again shall there be a flood to destroy the earth." (Gen. 9:9-11)

The flood experience in our individual lives means that we will experience cleansing situations, but nothing that happens to us can destroy us.

"This is the sign of the covenant which I make between me and you and every living creature that is with you, for all future generations: I set my bow in the cloud, and it shall be a sign of the covenant between me and the earth. When I

bring clouds over the earth and the bow is seen in the clouds, I will remember my covenant which is between me and you and every living creature of all flesh; and the waters shall never again become a flood to destroy all flesh. When the bow is in the clouds, I will look upon it and remember the everlasting covenant between God and every living creature of all flesh that is upon the earth. ... This is the sign of the covenant which I have established between me and all flesh that is upon the earth." (Gen. 9:12-17)

The words in chapter nine, verse eleven, seem to indicate that at some point in our evolution as individuals, and as the human family, we grew beyond the point of a possibility of our individuality ever being destroyed. The mysterious hint contained in these unexplained words of Scripture seem to express that at some point there may have been the possibility of cancelling out an individual on a particular life wave. However, evidently we "made it" in this life wave and are now in a state of indestructibility. It would be marvelous if this Scripture also included a statement that we were beyond damage, but that's not quite the truth *yet.* We have evolved into indestructible beings, yet we still experience clouds and floods, but nothing that can permanently harm us or destroy the reality of us, not even the so-called death experience!

What an insight into Truth realization! The Earth in Old Testament symbology represents the individual consciousness and the environment it is manifesting. Clouds represent dimming of the light, or the problems or challenges brought into everyone's life. You can't do without them right now! As the Earth needs clouds and their resulting rain to promote growth in nature, so do we. Thus, when a cloud rises over your horizon, know that you already have the perfect solution to the situation. *God is your help in every need.* And the presence and promise of God as the needed help, or the solution, is symbolized by the rainbow.

You are a conscious part of eternal life, and the coming in and going out of personal existence doesn't change your indestructibility. This is the first part of God's covenant or promise: Nothing can harm you permanently. Nothing can destroy your individual beingness. Expressed in another way, you are always greater than anything that might be happening. You are wondrously qualified and equipped to handle every life situation. "... *When the bow is in the clouds, I will look upon it and remember the everlasting covenant....*" This is God's part. It's already established. Now is the time to do your part. Through using your freedom of choice, through exercising your faculties of will and judgment, you can cooperate with God.

What's in the clouds?

All the different forms clouds can take are symbolic of the many varieties of challenges and "problem" situations that can occur. Some challenges (often called "stepping stones to growth" by Truth students; but call them what you will, they still have to be met and resolved!) are like the attractive white and fluffy clouds observed on a summer day. Other challenges are like the dark, rolling, opaque clouds analagous to storms. These represent the tougher decisions, requiring great understanding of the situation, and perhaps the answer is arrived at through deeper soul-searching.

Clouds bring the ingredients for rain to

bless and nourish the Earth. This is also true for life's various problems or challenges, for, in the overall scheme of things, they also bring meaningful factors for assisting one's spiritual growth. The problem itself doesn't give you a greater spiritual consciousness. But *how you handle the situation* can stimulate a marvelous growth experience. Should you find a seemingly maleficent cloud threatening to rain on your parade, look for God the good (the rainbow) in the situation.

The Light in the Rainbow

The promise of Scripture is that God has placed His rainbow *in advance* into any possible cloud that could overshadow any part of your personal earth. The rainbow is the God-Presence within you as all the potential right answers.

Now, the rainbow has all the perceptible colors, and yet, if that rainbow were not in a certain relationship to light, the colors wouldn't be visible. After all, the visible essence of the rainbow is light, not color, as some may think.

Colors are limitations manifesting under the vibratory law of pure light. These vibrations, as they strike the retina of the eye and certain brain parts, produce a sense of what is perceived as color. Colors are not self-existent. One person looking at someone in a business suit may state that the suit is blue, for that is the impression made upon his brain through his eyes, through the working of light. Another individual who is "color-blind" would not perceive the color blue.

I've read of blind persons who have had glimpses of movements or "sight" through their fingertips. I personally experienced a situation whereby a woman, blind from an accident at age twelve, began to regain her sight. At first she was unable to perceive pastel colors and had difficulty differentiating between blue and green. So, it is all relative. In analogy, each color of the spectrum then represents another possibility as a right answer or different alternative. Through your freedom of choice, you choose your favorite color of the moment which would be analogous to the right answer you perceive at a particular time.

Some folks think there's only one right answer for every problem. Life provides us greater leeway. A challenging situation may have a spectrum of appropriate answers. The "right" answer would not always consist of choosing "the right color," but doing the meaningful thing with the color (answer) you select.

Suppose there appear to be several alternatives to a problem. How do you know which one to select? All possibilities could be appropriate in different ways. The action then would be to pray for guidance for the awareness of the greater light. Take God into your decision, and that makes your choice the right one.

It's self-deception to think that progress and unfoldment are always straight-line infallibility. They aren't. The pathway follows cycles and recycles, spirals and more spirals, and perhaps a blind alley occasionally. Charles Fillmore reserved the right to change his mind in the face of new awareness. So can you!

We sometimes forget that a change of mind is often an important part of the outworking of the progression of a divine idea. The change of mind factor doesn't alter the Truth of inspired guidance and right decision.

Life is consciousness, my friends, and whatever you choose to do through your consciousness will produce its result in your expressions and manifestations of life. There is no such thing as a "right answer" to any situation without a mind, a person, and a heart to perceive it, formulate it, and express it.

So, to each his own insofar as which color of the rainbow is preferred at a given moment. The important thing to know is that *the rainbow is always present, and the omnipresence of God is a reality.*

How To Work the Rainbow Promises in Your Life

What is meant by the word "promise"? The Merriam-Webster Dictionary (1974) defines "promise" as a noun: . . . *a pledge to do or not to do something specified;* as a verb: . . . *likely to succeed or yield good results.*

The Scripture promises of God encompass all the aforementioned meanings and are part of your divine birthright as a beloved child of God. To receive the benefits of the promises, however, something is often required of you. *It is important that you claim these promises as your own. Have unshakable faith in their reality. And, take daily life action accordingly.*

Here are four basic steps for guidance in using the Scripture promises of God.

1. Accept each promise as it is *literally* given. Don't dissect it mentally or try to read between the lines. Have faith in what is given.

2. Command your thoughts and feelings to be still, and become open and receptive to the Truth that is presented.

3. If the promise requires action from you, be prepared to do your part willingly and lovingly. When Scripture tells you to "believe," then do so! God is always ready to do His part, and it is necessary for you to do yours.

4. The final step requires letting go and letting God work to fulfill the promise for your life in His wonderful way and appropriate time. Your answer may come at once. Then again, it may not. Don't get your feathers ruffled! God *will* keep His promise.

Take the time to read the Scripture references in your Bible in their chapter context. Get the complete story. When you find one promise to be especially meaningful, write it on a file card or memorize it so you will have it available for immediate reference. Know that what God promises, God fulfills!

You don't conceive of God being anything less than good do you? Well, you, having been made in the "image and likeness" of God, are also tremendous. You may not currently realize your greatness, and your friends and relatives may not believe it. Nevertheless, the spiritual pattern of God's ideal shines through you, confirming the Truth that you are perfect in Spirit. Perhaps you've only gotten "off track" in thoughts, feelings, and actions, and you feel somewhat alone. You're never alone, for: "...*lo, I am with you always*... (Matt. 28:20) is the promise.

Rainbow Meditation

"Awaken, O sleeper... and Christ shall give you light." (Eph. 5:14)

Living, loving Christ of my being, infinite, eternal, and creative Spirit of all, creative Source of all that I AM, You are the instant, constant, and abiding love, life, and energy of my being.

As I awaken increasingly to the Truth that You are shining within me always, I turn my attention from any and all appearances and disappearances of this world to all that is the same yesterday, today, and forever. I AM now recognizing and accepting that You are the Light of my world, that You are the radiating Intelligence and Wisdom and universal Love of my soul. I open my mind to radiant Light. All thoughts of doubt, darkness, and negation are dissolved and transmuted into faith, creative imagination, and understanding. All feelings of resentment and hatred are transmuted into an abiding aware-

ness of the oneness of all life and the harmonious expression of that oneness.

You are shining in my body as life. Old states of inertia, sluggishness, tension, and disease are eliminated, and I AM now alert, healthy, energetic, and strong. I AM whole. Praise God, I AM whole!

You are shining in my affairs as divine order, and all vestiges of lack, inharmony, injustice, and imbalance are brought lovingly into right relationship to You. Joy is restored in my life!

My mind, heart, body, and soul are in perfect alignment with You, my true Self. I easily move forth into my world to do that which needs to be done by me in joyous willingness to be about my Father's business of being an expression of the Light in the world that I AM in Spirit.

Thank You, God.

A Glorious Calculated Risk!

*A*s you seek to tap the unlimited potential that is your birthright as a child of God, you face the decision of taking a calculated risk! Now, relax your mind to an open and receptive state, and let's look at what is meant by "calculated risk." You will begin to understand why living a spiritually oriented life is taking a calculated risk, how you may accept this risk, and the glory of the unfolding soul that ensues.

The word *calculate* means: *To reckon by exercise or practical judgment; to design or adapt for a purpose. Risk means: To take a chance; to gamble.* A calculated risk means to determine through exercise of practical judgment (or discernment) to take a chance. Now, the word *chance* is sometimes defined as: *The unpredictable element in existence; opportunity.* One of the meanings of gamble is *to venture.* So, it seems there are two ways to risk or gamble. You can buy a lottery ticket on the unpredictable possibility that you may win a fortune, or a country can stake vast sums of money and the lives of several persons on the uncertain event that the first space shuttle, the Columbia, will pave the way for great scientific advances in America's space program. The lottery ticket is a *risk*. The space program is a *calculated risk*. Of course, you may try to convince yourself that anything you do which departs from your daily mien is a risk, and that line of thinking gets you absolutely nowhere!

You may ask why, then, is living a spiritually oriented life a calculated risk? Look around you at what's happening in your world each day. If you are facing a problem situation, an intense personal relationship, or change in some form, and the whole experience looms large and complicated, what positive assurance do you have that everything will unfold harmoniously and successfully?

Here's where God's promises provide needed encouragement. As you apply the Truth principles you know, pray affirmatively, practice daily meditation, hold your thoughts and feelings positive, and speak constructively, definite good results must occur. When you put the universal laws to work, launch time arrives! Neither you nor I may be able to predict the exact point in time, or the exact manner in which the situation will be perfectly resolved. That's the calculated risk. However, all effort brings results!

Scripture tells us in Mark 9:23: "... *All things are possible to him who believes.*" We are aware of our faculty of faith through Charles Fillmore's tremendous book *The Twelve Powers of Man.* Faith is our trust without reservation. We have faith that the seasons of the year will follow each other in orderly progression. We have faith that the sun will burst forth in celestial glory each morning, whether we see it or not. And we have faith in our body functions of heartbeat, breathing, digestion, and so on. Oh, the beauty of faith! How powerful it is! Thoughts, words, and actions are outlets, or vehicles, through which the very essence of life is expressed. And faith in God and the outworking of universal law is the standard from which it is lived.

If a farmer sowed thistle seeds and then complained that his field failed to yield him wheat, you might comment, "What a foolish man! If he wanted wheat, why didn't he plant wheat?" The law of "as you sow, so shall you reap" is constantly outpicturing. The farmer planting wheat has the inner knowing that his calculations of harvesting an abundant crop are good. He does the necessary work of planting and tending the crop. Nature activates the risk-factor through the ensuing sunshine and rain. The promise is fulfilled in God's time as the wheat harvest. A predetermined goal is accomplished. The same love energy is at work whether the situation is overcoming illness, changing jobs, resolving a financial crisis, surviving a divorce, or planting a wheat crop!

First Steps to Overcoming

I've often thought of Jesus' life at home with His family, meeting the day-to-day activities with the monotony and unwavering usualness that we, too, experience. Surely one of the lessons every student learns is that of working in harmony with the family group, however large or small it may be. For some, this means taking some calculated risks along the growth process journey. Until divinity is expressed in the home and among family members and friends, how can we expect to demonstrate this attainment elsewhere? *It is vitally important to live as children of God in the setting in which we are placed.* I'm reminded of a statement often seen on greeting cards, wall hangings, and decorative plaques which says: *Bloom where you are planted!* This is exactly what we are to do. *The place where we are is the starting point from which our journey begins.* And thought of "escape" from a place, a person, or a situation is like looking *through a glass darkly.* (I Cor. 13:12 A.V.) As an understanding of the spiritual principles we presently perceive is demonstrated by living the Truth daily, then life will offer the opportunity to advance and grow in other areas. Now is the time for self-discipline. Herein lies the self-testing and the positive overcoming!

Many sincere students feel they could make an impression on their immediate surroundings and manifest divinity if they lived in a different kind of home or neighborhood, drove a better car, had more money in the bank and more leisure time, associated with "better" friends, or enjoyed good physical health. Why, there's no telling what could be accomplished, if . . . !

Repeatedly we're told by teachers, books, music, and various forms of expression that, as children of God, we embarked on this journey of life fully equipped with every tool required to live successfully in all ways. This knowledge narrows the percentage of risk, so why don't we believe God's promises and use what we have?

As we begin to truly open our eyes and "see," it becomes apparent that we have exactly those circumstances and the environment in which the lessons in obedience to divine Principle can be learned from the highest degree.

Oh, man, know thyself! We have the appropriate contacts in the world and the proper work required to propel us forward upon the path of overcoming and regeneration. Until the path of life is trodden in an aspiring, happy, positive, and expectant state of awareness, in the silent communion with Spirit which allows no self-pity or woe-is-me attitude, no new golden door of opportunity will swing wide in welcome.

It is imperative to understand that we are responsible for the difficulties encountered through our thoughts, feelings, and actions. Antagonism can be invoked from those around us through the action and fact of spiritual selfishness. For example, ask yourself, "Is it necessary that family or associates recognize my private time of prayer and meditation? Do I demand total quiet in the home or office?" Perhaps some of the difficulties would be eliminated if the aspirant remembered two important facts. First, prayer and meditation time is a process carried on silently, regularly, and in the secret place of the Most High within the individual. The Master said: "... *when you pray, go into your room and shut the door and pray to your Father who is in secret; and your Father who sees in secret will reward you.*" (Matt. 6:6) Second, how much more would be accomplished if the desire to be a Horatio Hornblower were released! It is important to walk silently with God, to hold the reins on the human personality, and keep the ego in the background. Place importance upon living life in such a way that due time is given to the culture of your soul. The results of such work cannot be hidden!

Through love we initiate ourselves in life, and from that point of beginning we ensure obedience to the highest that is within us. From the center point of universal love we gain confidence in the power of the indwelling Christ and demonstrate our growth through a life of loving service. Is this not what Jesus meant when He extended the unparalleled invitation: *"Follow me"?* (Matt. 9:9) And is not the first great step toward overcoming applying the strength and daring to put Truth principles to work in your life?

The Law of the Lamp

Almost everyone is familiar with the story of Aladdin and his wonderful lamp. A marvelous genie, who eagerly awaited Aladdin's bidding, lived in the lamp. Yet, in the fable, the genie didn't simply appear whenever Aladdin wished. He had to *do something* to invoke the genie's presence. Aladdin had to rub the lamp! When Aladdin took the necessary steps for putting into action the proper process for something to happen, his good appeared. This same activity is true for us!

Begin now to use the attributes you already possess, whether they are talents and abilities, material possessions now owned, or fantastic opportunities for service to yourself and to others. *Do the most you know how to do with what you have to do with!*

Take one step at a time; and begin by taking the step immediately ahead of you. Rub your lamp! Clear the way in your consciousness and in your life for the abundant good you earnestly desire. It's amazing that when we peruse the miraculous demonstrations of prosperity recounted in the Old and New Testaments, we recognize that simple, everyday things are used. For example, David slew the giant Goliath with a small pebble hurled from a slingshot! Elijah called forth great abundance to meet a widow's daily needs by using the small amount of oil she had available! Jacob obtained a superb dower from his father-in-law Laban by intelligently using some spotted willow sticks! Joseph mastered his dungeon in Egypt and became an "overnight" success as second in command to Pharoah. Jesus broke five loaves and two fishes and fed a multitude of five thousand persons. I could go on and on. All these people had one thing in common:

They proved that any picture held firmly in mind must come forth as a tangible result in its own way and in its own time!

If You Think You Can, You Can!

This Truth was deeply impressed upon me through an experience in my own life. Since early childhood, a strong, undeniable urge to write lived as closely as my shadow. While a sophomore in high school, I wrote my first book! It was about something I loved greatly at the time, horses, and I poured my loving thoughts and feelings onto what seemed to be reams of paper. Of course, my English teacher rewarded me with a fabulous grade and loads of encouragement! Enthusiasm soared! I wrote steadily and profusely, perhaps a lot of which was mediocre.

I continued writing. Several years passed, and I became an executive in a furniture manufacturing company as director of advertising and public relations. Here were more opportunites to write. Ideas for "happy" articles began pouring through my mind, and a newspaper column manifested, but not without effort! I had to *rub the lamp!*

One morning, bold as brass, and with more courage than good sense, I strolled into the local newspaper office and proclaimed that I wanted to write free-lance articles for the paper. Believing in being prepared, I produced several sample articles and submitted them to the editor. In stunned amazement at the intrusion into his office, the editor stared at me, then reached out and took the articles and glanced through them. Our eyes met and held for a moment or two. He shook his head, handed the articles back to me, and said, "We don't run this stream-of-consciousness type of article. Now, if you want a job as a reporter, you've got it!"

"No," I replied. "I have a job. I want to be a writer." So, I promptly gathered myself together and went to the competitive weekly paper. As I sat before this editor while he looked at my work, I visualized him surrounded in dazzling white light, and I saw mentally my articles in print each week and bringing favorable comments to his paper from his readers.

After about five minutes and a lot of paper-shuffling on his desk, he heaved a deep sigh and said, "Okay, tell you what. We will experiment! We will accept your articles on a weekly basis. You will submit each article one week in advance and, if accepted, you will have an article published in our paper each Thursday evening."

"Will I have a byline?" I asked.

He shrugged. "Why not! The whole idea's crazy anyway. We've nèver run this type of thing before!"

Two weeks later my articles began appearing in the newspaper. Within a month, letters were starting to reach the editor's desk with positive comments from people who looked forward to reading some good news in the paper. I continued to write the column for two years and, in addition, wrote several full-page specials.

So, you see, the law of the lamp works! But it is important for us to rub our lamps in order for the genie to appear!

A Divine Prescription for Risk Taking

The activity of God is a divine prescription that will enrich the life and experience of everyone who takes it. When accepted in faith, the divine prescription will multiply the blessings of a rich and successful life, bring new direction and meaning to a complacent one, revitalize a monotonous one, and completely transform one that is beset by problems of any kind.

However, before you take this divine prescription, here's a word of caution: Even a halfhearted acceptance of the powerful Truth contained in this formula will *permanently alter your outlook on life, your understanding of yourself, your relationship with God, and*

*lead you into experiences of living that will
cause you to grow mentally, emotionally, and
in every other way!*

The divine prescription is a sure thing in
overcoming because it works in three action-
packed sections:

1. It states Truth simply.
2. It describes the action of Truth in
   your life.
3. It tells the result of the action of
   Truth in your life.

The power of this effective prescription lies
not in the words alone, but also in the power
of the Truth the words contain. However, the
words themselves serve a wonderful and in-
dispensable purpose: they direct your attention to the Truth they contain, and they help
you to advance your attitude of faith and ex-
pectancy which, in turn, leads to your *knowing* Truth. As the Master said: "... *you will
know the truth, and the truth will make you
free.*" (John 8:32) This means freedom from
every type of limitation, be it mental, physical, emotional, or habitual.

Here's your prescription:

*The activity of God is the only power at
work in my mind, heart, and life. All false
beliefs, all negative appearances are dis-*

solved right now by the loving, forgiving action of God. I am whole, strong, and free as God created me to be.

Accept this divine prescription in your mind. Memorize the words, but don't stop there. Meditate on the Truth proclaimed by the words. Digest and assimilate them mentally and emotionally until the words themselves gather the faith, love, and energy always present in your God-created soul into a rainbow reservoir of light ready for use!

Let's look at the three sections more closely. First, the Truth is stated: *The activity of God is the only power at work in my mind, heart, and life.* Simple and direct! There is one Presence and one Power at work in all the universe. God! Therefore, there is one activity which is the creative, loving, energetic, eternal action that brought the universe into being, including you, and that sustains it throughout eternity. As you meditate upon the Truth involved, your capacity for understanding begins to expand. This statement is presented to your faith faculty, for those who would experience the activity of God in their lives must first believe that it exists and is responsive to their call.

The next section of the prescription states:

All false beliefs, all negative appearances are dissolved right now by the loving, forgiving action of God.

What a relief and release to begin to *know* this great reality, and what changes it makes in our prayers and meditations. How easy it is to block the expressions of the activity of God in our lives by allowing false beliefs in other powers such as the negative appearance of fear, condemnation, guilt, resentment, doubt, inertia, complacency, and unhappiness that these beliefs produce to inhabit our minds. They are like short circuits in an electric power line. They are the obstacles that distort and block the flow of the divine energy which is always moving in, through, and around us.

The action results in the process of happening! *I am whole, strong, and free as God created me to be* is the natural result of the action of Truth. The divine prescription works in you. It works to transform your world through you. When you know yourself to be whole, strong, and free as God created you to be, you then become a mighty center of divine power to successfully handle every situation of which you are a part.

The divine prescription can be a general or

a specific remedy. It can be taken for body, mind, finances, human relationships, healing, and rejuvenation. In fact, it is a powerful unguent for every human need. I've seen its great miracle-working power enrich many lives, especially mine! Remember, the divine prescription is a calculated risk, and from your studies in Truth, you have a pretty good idea what the results will be!

The Advancing Human Soul

As human souls grow and develop, they become increasingly interested in their fellow human beings who endure the joys and sorrows, successes and strifes, health and suffering brought about by the ever-active universal law of cause and effect. Advancing human souls empathize with their fellow travelers and try to cheer and encourage those whom they meet. Every firm handclasp that is offered in assistance brings a greater humbleness in the joy of true and selfless service. These evolving children of God long for more and deeper illumination and wisdom. Hatred and vengeance begin to fade from their evolving consciousness, and they increasingly realize that true justice ultimately prevails.

Ascending spiritually sparks the understanding of the necessity of life on Earth—this earthly existence enables such souls to purify and evolve in *direct proportion* to their love and compassion and transmutation of any negatives that may remain in them. The advancing human soul uses regularly the keys of experience and discernment—of themselves and of their fellowmen—to solve unknown mysteries.

Advancing human souls learn to recognize the masks covering the faces of many of their fellow travelers. In such persons, the expression of the eyes often fails to agree with the set of the mouths. They use cosmetics—material and emotional—to hide the wrinkles that depict years of suffering, anxiety, struggle, hardship, and, yes, joy and progression. A downturned mouth attempts to smile, but the glow of inner happiness does not sparkle in eyes which are dull and lackluster.

What a vast amount of experience lies hidden behind the eyes of a reincarnated human being. This is a secret known only to him whom Spirit carries along into the cosmos, moving the advancing souls ever nearer to new and happier lives, closer to the light of God.

Advancing human souls know that the greatest antidote for any seeming lack, limitation, or negative experience is to count their blessings daily. It is impossible for anyone to be aware of abundance present in life and to feel deprived at the same time. Regardless of any situation that may be present, the factor of life—God-life moving through all—brings cause for thanksgiving and rejoicing. How else could one become the master over the earth plane of matter without God?

Break free, advancing human souls, from all self-imposed bondage! Unshakable faith and the courage to do what some may term "impossible" will make you leaders. Advancing human souls see what is necesssary and know that a new day always follows the night. They understand that only in appearances could anything be impossible. Their positive attitudes provide the inner assurance and sustenance that rise victorious over any circumstance.

The more advancing human souls expect and demand of themselves in life's performance and achievement, the greater are their accomplishments. This is the truth about advancing human souls. You are infinitely greater than you think!

Check yourself out! Look at all your hopes and dreams, your aspirations, your faith in your abilities. Who knows what great possibilities of immense accomplishments are in store for you. Another rainbow promise says: *... he who sows sparingly will also reap sparingly, and he who sows bountifully will also reap bountifully.* (II Cor. 9:6)

Rainbow Meditation

Relax. See yourself enfolded in the golden light of illumination. No risk is involved when you reach to the light which is within and springing from divine love, which is universal feeling that transcends every human concept. The rainbow rays of scintillating light weave a pattern of peace, harmony, and mastery that transmutes all human discord, struggle, limitation, and irritation.

Claim your radiant feeling of life.

Be the masterful manifestation and dominion through the light over all things material. Acknowledge now the Truth that you are the Presence of God-life in action now.

As you acknowledge the presence of divine love, the door swings wide to the light within its heart which is the Gift, the Giver, and the eternal Power of all that you desire.

Talk to your flesh body. Inform it: I am the Presence of the light of divine love flowing in and through this flesh body, permeating every atom, cell, and electron with life energy, and illuminating my pathway wherever I desire to travel. I am an advancing soul.

I open my heart now to the God within, seeking always that sincerity of purpose which means I am constant and true to my inner self and eliminate error and unnecessary risks from my activities.

I seek to be pure in heart, clear in mind, strong and healthy in body, unshakable in faith, and attuned with the secret place of the Most High.

I am at peace. I work in the silence of my daily life, doing all I can to contribute to universal life the love and wisdom from my indwelling Christ Presence.

Be Thou Made Whole!

*T*he counselee sitting across from me paused in giving a dissertation of his "superior" knowledge. He exhibited great pride in his extensive education, and wielded his knowledge mightily for ego satisfaction. He displayed his intellect in conversation as a merchant displays goods in a shop window. His self-image was that of an intellectual, a thinker; yet, in reality, he was like a mechanical man, loaded with vanity and arrogance. And woe to the person who dared to point it out! He had knowledge but he did not *know*. He needed healing, but he did not know how to accept and receive it.

Knowledge is a necessary ingredient in life. But you can't bake a cake with only flour! Use your knowledge and allow it to jolt you out of old and crystallized habits and you'll uncover an essential healing ingredient: the *willingness to face yourself in actuality*. This willingness eventually eliminates the false pride of having knowledge, which then releases that knowledge to operate on a higher, more effective level.

How many times have you prayed for healing and didn't receive it in the manner you wished? Why? Was the reason a lack of manifested faith? Or, perhaps, it was lack of preparedness to assume the responsibility for health. Did you fail to forgive someone who may have caused you harm; did you hold tightly to a grudge?

Some persons ask why saints and spiritual leaders sometimes have serious illnesses. Don't they know the principles of healing? Isn't a devout person spiritual enough to be whole and well?

We just cannot judge what is in another person's consciousness. The soul may be using health challenges or handicaps as stepping-stones to make giant strides in growth. Helen Keller's physical blindness was naught in comparison to the greatness of her *true* vision. Ludwig van Beethoven closed his physical ears to worldly clamor and opened his inner ears to proclaim the celestial "music of the spheres" for the entire universe to hear! How often we tend to jump to conclusions. If a principle doesn't seem to be working, perhaps the reason is that we haven't correctly understood the mechanism. *That which is real always works!*

There once lived, in an Indian village, a simple man whose healing prayers were always answered. He became well-known in the countryside surrounding his village, and many people brought their healing prayer requests to him. They asked, "How is it that your prayers are always answered?" The man replied, "I believe in the healing power of the Great Spirit." But the villagers couldn't imagine the situation was that ordinary. So, they sent a small boy to spy on the man. Day after day the boy carefully observed the man's actions. Every day, about six a.m., the man would emerge from his small home, face the east, and stretch his arms heavenward. Catching sight of his goat nearby, the man would then catch the goat and tie it to a tree. The goat would then nibble on the low-hanging branches. The boy reported this information to the leaders of the village: "All you have to do to get your prayers answered is to get a goat and go out at six a.m. each day . . . !"

This story humorously portrays the necessity to attune to the Truth about healing and spend life's precious time working toward a consciousness of wholeness, rather than being sidetracked by useless details.

There is not one atom or cell of your being that does not have God's presence and power. When you are fully aware of this Truth, regeneration, or Christ consciousness, begins to take place.

A Healing Revelation

What is this activity called healing? The study of Truth reveals to us that healing is the process of restoring to original purity or integrity. The first step in this process is to believe healing can be accomplished, and the second step is to become open and receptive in thought and feeling to constructive new healing ideas and techniques.

All healing is based on mental cleansing. As you release error thoughts from your mind, harmony begins to reign in your body. Some persons spend large amounts of money and take huge quantities of medicines to cure various aches and pains. However, *permanent healing* isn't accomplished until the *mental cause* of the dis-ease, the error thought, is removed.

Do you believe deep within yourself that a pill or injection will ward off disease and death? Do you think you are completely alone simply because another person isn't with you? Think further. Look deeper. See clearer. A problem cannot be solved until you know there is a problem, and know the nature of the problem. Often the body's suffering is a mask the mind wears to camouflage the real *cause* of the suffering.

Look again at the Truth about yourself. Your body is a lovely temple, wonderfully wrought, designed for intricate functioning. It is the temple for life eternal, and every cell in your body has the ingrained ability to radiate abundant light, love, happiness, health, and serenity. As this activity is allowed to manifest, you enjoy the perfect health that is yours by divine right. The joy of living emanates from you, and you can project this spirit of wholeness into every area of your world.

What you think about everything in your life affects your health, wealth, affairs, and happiness.

What you think about yourself, life, death, health, prosperity, the universe; what you think about your husband or wife, children, work associates, neighbors, friends, relatives; what you think about personal affairs, and what you think about world affairs, affect you! Every thought that passes through your mind affects your success, health, and prosperity in life.

If your life seems restricted, there can be release from the limited world you have made. You are assured through promises of God, that ... *the kingdom of God is within you* (Luke 17:21 A.V.) and, therefore, cannot be limited.

Confused thinking causes confused living experiences and mistakes. Confused emotions result in seeming failure. When you allow confusion to enter your thinking, problems tend to overwhelm you and often lead to a scattering of your life energy which, in turn, can lead to more problems.

Whatever emotions you might be feeling, try to let them be guided by an awareness of God's love and beauty. All emotions, to some degree, are an attempt on the part of the individual to express a divine idea.

Your subconscious mind is susceptible. It believes everything you tell it! And it has absolutely no sense of humor! When you tell your subconscious mind that the body temple it calls home is sick or hurting, your body temple may suffer the consequences of disease and pain.

But there is hope! You can refuse to accept error thinking. Every word you speak, every thought you think, every desire you feel, sets into motion certain vibrations. These vibrations are sensed by your intuition. Using intuition, you can command through the spoken word the energy of spiritual vibrations to raise your consciousness and bring calm to any troubled waters in your life. People don't fail in their quests for greater enlightenment because they lack intelligence. Failure, instead, is more often the result of one's refusal to take advantage of what is being offered.

Each person—whatever his social or business standing—be he a materialist, an idealist, or a mystic, must check the foundation of his theories through sincere examination of his conscience to determine any area of consciousness where housecleaning is necessary. The evolving person, upon attaining a certain expression of light, will never utter an unkind word to judge another, will forgive any offence and, yes, will love even his enemies!

True mysticism springs from within and is

actually the conviction to give oneself, without restriction, in service to God and humanity, and to help substantiate the divine plan on Earth. It is the most exalted condition a human being is able to reach.

Speak the Word of Health

When did you last tell your body how much you appreciate the years of effective service it has given you? Did you take time this morning to bless every limb, muscle, bone, and cell of your wonderful body? Did you remind it that it is a marvelous reservoir of abundant life and energy, that divine order and wholeness are active in every nerve, cell, and organ? If you didn't, you are neglecting your precious body and your responsibility to it! And if something so vital and necessary is neglected, how do you expect it to perform satisfactorily? You wouldn't fail to service and maintain your car. You wouldn't want the inconvenience of it not working! Your body, the temple you use twenty-four hours a day, is much more important!

When we don't take time or make the effort to maintain our body vehicles, they suffer as a result. The body can become weak and depleted, and pain can occur. This is the body's way of telling us that we are neglecting it. The body does not act completely of its own accord. It cannot feed itself. It depends upon you. It cannot spring out of bed in the morning and brush its teeth. That is your job! It cannot move an arm or a leg without your will or desire. Jesus spoke healing words with power and effectiveness. You have the mastery to do the same.

We are spiritual beings, living in physical bodies, experiencing on a plane of matter. Yet, we have power and authority over the physical body. It is time we assume this mastery and accept the responsibility of working with the physical body in the proper ways. We are old souls living throughout eternity, expressing through many bodies. Thus, we are more important than our bodies in a particular incarnation, or what happens to those bodies. But this physical vehicle is vitally important, and when it is not kept in good health, it burdens us with pain and limitation. And where is the joy in restriction?

Ask yourself, "Do I really want to be well and stay that way? If so, what am I willing to do about it?" Jesus came upon a man by Bethzatha pool in Jerusalem who had been lame since birth. Jesus asked the man: *"Do you want to be healed?"* (John 5:6) That seems a strange question to ask a man who had spent his life experiencing illness, but the question isn't as unusual as it may seem. The meaning behind the question was: Do you actually will to be well? Are you ready to take command of the forces within yourself and accept a healing? If you do not sincerely *will* it, then you cannot claim it!

The man answered, *"Sir, I have no man to put me into the pool...."* (John 5:7) He wanted to place the blame on someone else, when all the time he could have taken important action for himself had he known what to do.

Sickness sometimes comes from an unconscious will to be sick, failure from a will to fail, poverty from a will to lack. This happens subtly, perhaps, for some people don't realize they unconsciously use a condition or a problem to get attention from loved ones, which to them is more important than getting well.

Health of body is our normal state of being. *It is naturally ours unless it is blocked by fears, stresses, strains, or wrong beliefs that produce dis-ease.*

The result of your thinking and feeling is

your consciousness, and you are a personification of your own consciousness. In other words, *thinking plus feeling equals demonstration.* Thus, you develop your consciousness and it becomes the creator of your body and your world, just as you are the creator of your consciousness. Since it is *your* consciousness that forms your body and your world, when you desire a better body or world it is necessary to change your consciousness for the better. This means to substitute light in the place of darkness, health in the place of sickness, life rather than death, and raising your overall attitude from negative to positive expression.

Understanding the Term "Error Consciousness"

The "mortal mind," or the mind of the flesh, is the error consciousness which gathers its information from the outside world through the five senses and can produce erroneous thinking. The mind of the flesh allows us to believe in sickness, death, and sorrow, but the mind of Spirit has the ability to transform this error consciousness and convey the Truth of health and happiness, and eternal life.

It is important to be careful of moods and feelings, for there is a connection between these moods and feelings and the visible world. The body is an emotional filter and bears the marks of prevalent thoughts and feelings.

The control of error consciousness leads to knowledge of the real Self, and the knowledge of the Self, or the I AM, or God-man, or however you identify the supreme part of your soul, leads to greater control of consciousness. Such control must necessarily involve the discipline of the senses, mind, and heart, as well as harnessing of one's energies. This is accomplished through correct applications of Truth principles in daily living.

Through your five senses of seeing, tasting, smelling, touching, and hearing, you function in the outer or material world, while your inner or spiritual world is felt and understood through the inner aspects of all your senses and functions. It is the use of the inner aspects of your senses and functions that constitutes your intuition. Intuition is the "inner knowledge," the "knower," the still, small voice within, your own invisible channel, connecting you directly with God. It is the Holy Spirit speaking lovingly to your soul. It is a direct and absolute knowing, although no intellectual reason may be apparent. When you are aware of all these aspects of your being, and you refuse to accept error-thinking, you get *results!*

"You will seek me and find me; when you seek me with all your heart, I will be found by you . . . ." (Jer. 29:13, 14)

There is no situation in which God cannot be found, for He is the one Presence and the one Power. Naturally, the result of persistently seeking God in every situation is that we find Him, along with all the attributes of His love.

Remember, nothing can arrive in the outer that has not first come as a thought in mind. You might say, "Oh, I wouldn't think such a thing!" This statement may be correct insofar as a specific condition is concerned. However, whenever you let your thinking dwell on anything of a negative nature, something that does not accord with the Truth of your being as a child of God, the inevitable results appear. *As in mind, so in manifestation.*

Be Thou Made Whole!

The Message of a Master

The healing at Cana of the son of a courtier of Capernaum as described in John 4:46-54 was the second work performed by Jesus publicly. (The first event was the changing of water into wine.)

What prompted the nobleman to believe that his son, who was at the point of death, could be healed by Jesus? There was no record of Jesus having done healing work before. There was no reason for this nobleman to connect Jesus with healing if we consider the literal, historical translation of Scripture. Is it not logical to assume that this individual, in his desire for help for his son, reaffirmed the superconscious level of his own mind and received an increase in consciousness, which increase enabled him to have broader understanding and perception? Then he encountered Jesus, and his intuition informed him that Jesus could help.

We cannot understand the healing activity of Jesus' ministry by taking an isolated incident and trying to squeeze the secret from it. Rather, it seems that each incident in Jesus' healing ministry contains a special point for awareness, a special kind of instruction directed to the particular healing need. No single healing miracle contains the entirety of healing. The reading of the healing words and works of Jesus creates a cumulative effect and realization that in each instance He brought forth another aspect of what is called "the healing consciousness."

The message of healing is spread over the whole of the Gospels, and we gather and absorb these different points that Jesus made, not taking each one out of context, but by viewing the entirety of His healing ministry.

Jesus did not teach how to heal; rather, He outlined the ingredients needed for acceptance and incorporation into individual consciousness to build the healing consciousness.

The first step in building a healing consciousness is to believe in the divine idea of health, which makes healing possible . . . the divine idea of life and wholeness, and add to that God's will-to-good for every person.

Scripture says in Joshua 24:15: "... *choose this day whom you will serve* ...." Do you believe in the inevitability and permanence of sickness? Or, do you believe in the divine idea of health and wholeness?

The Healing Power of Love

In Divine Mind, love is the expression of universal unity flowing throughout creation. Love is the magnificent, magnetic, attracting, and harmonizing power that enfolds everything in perfect order.

We grasp some comprehension of love as it is clothed in form. We see love manifested as tender compassion between husband and wife, the close relationship between mother and child, or devoted service for a cause believed in.

We can see love manifested in creation by observing the divine order of the universe. The relationship of our sun, moon, the stars, planets, flowers, trees, seas, and mountains are all expressions of love manifesting through Divine Mind.

Guatama Buddha said: *To give five minutes to the realization of true divine love is greater than to pass a thousand bowls of food to the needy, because in giving forth love, you help every soul in the universe!* And Jesus said: *"You shall love the Lord your God with all your heart, and with all your soul, and with all your mind. ... You shall love your neighbor as yourself."* (Matt. 22:37, 39)

57

Love, love, love! Use it bountifully for radiant health. The more you use, the more you shall have to use. Love is that part of Himself that God has placed into every living thing.

The Direct Road to Healing

The direct road to healing is through spiritual attainment. Constantly turn your thoughts inward toward the presence of the Christ in you, your hope of glory, and let them dwell on the good within all. Direct your "mind of the flesh" to be still and let that mind that is God (all-love, all-wisdom) think in you and through you.

Use positive words and thoughts in everything you do. Plant within your soul the perfect seed idea. Ask to manifest only the outworkings of this perfect seed idea, to radiate perfect health, to express perfect harmony, and to realize perfect abundance—not to be delivered from inharmony, misery, and limitations. Throw these effects off as you would discard a worn-out garment. They are old and outgrown ideas and you can discard them joyfully. Don't give them a passing glance as they are released. All is forgiven and released. They have returned to the dust from

which they were created. They are no-thing.
Nothing.

Fill in the seemingly blank spaces around
you with the thought of God, infinite Good.
Then remember the word "God" is a seed. It
must grow. Leave the how and the when and
the where to God. Your role is to say what
you want, and to give forth blessings, knowing that the moment you have asked, you
have received, which is another promise.
"... *ask, and you will receive, that your joy
may be full.*" (John 16:24) Ask! Affirm! Look
to God for your spiritual attainment; then receive fulfillment.

Seven Basic Steps for Developing
a Healing Consciousness

1. Make a commitment to health and
   wholeness. Select a definite starting
   point, such as the ideas of peace, oneness, awareness. Use an affirmation
   to guide the flow of attention so you
   may come to a realization of that
   which you seek and speak. It is yours
   to claim now. Affirm:
   *I commit my thoughts, feelings,
   and actions to the divine idea of*

health and wholeness in my being. I open my mind now to an expanded awareness of perfection. I feel this activity taking place within me now, and I am grateful. I release everything that does not contribute to the outpicturing of God's divine plan for my life.

2. Relax completely. Take a deep breath, slowly inhaling and exhaling to relax your thought vibrations. Begin at the top of your head and direct universal energy slowly through your body with a visualization of healing light cascading around you.

3. Realize the presence and power of God within you. Relax into deeper God-awareness. Relax into the tranquillity of the divine idea of oneness with God. Blend completely into the one Presence and Power in your thoughts and feelings.

4. Feel the activity of God within you. Feel yourself flowing deeper into a feeling of perfection. Become aware of your body. Feel the healing energy in the cells of your body. The process you are using is moving from a con-

cept of thinking to a feeling of the Truth of the action of rainbow light in your body.

5. Picture the healing. Let your audible affirmation become a quiet whisper. Should your attention wander, refocus it on an image of perfect wholeness, using your faculty of will to accomplish this.

6. Accept the mental picture of wholeness. This is the realization within your own being. It is not self-delusion. *Healing is the Truth about yourself.* You began with an idea, moved into an imaging, experienced the feeling, and now you accept the realization in your body.

7. Give thanks! The mental picture and the feeling are now permanent parts of your consciousness. The result is a growing consciousness of health which releases the life-force, brings prompt healing, and regulates the vital forces of your body.

The Promises of God

The promises of God are certain, eternal,

unalterable. The life spark of God within us is our promise and great invitation to lay claim to all good. Spirit is Cause and Source, and when we return to the Source, we are regenerated. We are not only sound in mind, but sound in body and affairs, for our entire being is united into that great unity which is the essential nature of all things. We are the oneness of the whole. We are virtual centers of living unity!

When Jesus said: "... *he who believes in me will also do the works that I do; and greater works than these will he do...*" (John 14:12) He was speaking from the consciousness of the only true unity, the soundness of each individual in our relationship to and with the creator. And since God is Good and all His creations are perfect and good, then His laws operate in this perfection, and we realize all His "promises" come true and are real.

One of the "secrets" of Jesus' power was in His complete reliance upon what He felt moving in this deepest nature and which He called the Father within. The law (promise) of God is written in the divine archetype of each person, and to outwardly obey that which is moving within is to bring the inner capacity into outer manifestation. God has made the human soul to develop like a seed planted in the soil to quicken and sprout. He injected this seed with an atom of life sparked with a yearning for evolution. The human being harbors a soul gifted with reason but must be trained to become a sensitive entity and work to find his or her way to purification and redemption. That which moves in the deepest side of our nature is the inward action of the universal Principle and the true promise of God.

Rainbow Meditation

Creative Source!
Peace . . . Peace . . . all is peace.
From the deep well of the soul, the pouring
    forth of the great peace
Is my consent within body as well as in mind
    to Thy perfect will.
Give me, today, an awareness of thy presence
    within.
I seek to feel the effusion of healing love
    flooding over the
Precious opening of my heart from the Heart
    of hearts.
Forgive me any feeling of separation,
And I shall forgive and love those who feel
    separated from me.
Bring into my beingness the wave of healing
    radiation from
The rainbow covenant. Sweep it before
    everything in my nature
That is negative and destructive.
Wash away and cleanse, burn out and

dissolve
All error thinking.
Deliver me from ignorance so that I
    experience a complete change
In the wake of the radiant soul-fire
From destruction through man
To construction through man,
Creating and establishing the will for the
    peace of the
Flesh, the mind, the soul.
All through my being now surges the
    emanation of this power of God.
For Thou, within me, are perfect harmony,
    all-powerful love,
And the joy of life eternal.
And so it is!

The Song of Songs

*H*ow important and how good it is to open your mind and heart to the God presence within. Seek always to be true to your inner self. Analyze your motives daily and search diligently for any sign of selfish desire or impure action. If you would glean a rich understanding of the ancient wisdom—and this knowledge is the basis of many teachings—you must be pure in heart and willing to work in the secret place of the Most High. Jesus stressed this in His teaching promise: "... *and your Father who sees in secret will reward you.*" (Matt. 6:4) That which seems hidden shall one day be shouted from the rooftops. Be at peace. Work and contribute to universal life in your daily expression of love, and wisdom shall be abundantly revealed to you as you commune with the Most High.

Great teachers of the past have always gone to a high place to receive God's commands. They quietly withdrew from the swarming multitudes, from the noise and clamor of their surroundings, and ascended in consciousness to receive from the infinite creative Source the refreshment that enabled them to return to their daily world and its requirements. Their bodies were refreshed and revitalized by the cosmic life stream which flows from the Fountainhead, and which pours forth life essence upon all creatures, great and small, in this world. Remember, *the Source of the human life stream is the place of the Most High, the mountaintop!*

The Pure in Heart Shall See God

Purity and sincerity of purpose flow as sparkling streams from the foundation of true divine love, bringing the unity of all. God is great. We are God's children, and we can partake of His greatness. When the great light of Truth shines from the altar of our innermost being, we can truly participate in the simplicity, the purity, and the greatness of God, our Creator.

Each of us has been given the power to increase the light of God on Earth. The Truth beams forth from God to touch the hearts of all Earth brethren, so greater spiritual light may illumine the path of each person. The light of the Christ continually falls upon us but does not easily penetrate our minds, because of our free will. We are free to tune in either to the light of the Christ or to the darkness of our own material-plane reasoning. If we desire our light to shine forth, to bring illumination to the darkness, we must use our precious faculty of free will to make the decision to attune our whole being with the light.

Take the light with you wherever you go. Take it to work. Take it to church. Take it to visit a neighbor or a friend. Wear it as a smile each day. Let it abide in your heart and radiate throughout your daily experiences. It is easy to be cheerful when conditions are harmonious and the outer plane warrants it; but the cheerful heart works harder when the Earth is shrouded in darkness. Yet, it is this very time, when the light grows dim, that we are tested. It is easy to be kind when others are kind. It is easy to be loving when others praise our good works. Blessed is the one who stands strong and true moment by moment, hour by hour, day by day, under all circumstances.

A wise person who knows that the sun is

always shining and that when darkness seems to be upon the face of the Earth (the human consciousness), it will be only a little earthly time before the darkness vanishes as the dawn comes. While time may seem to be a great limiting factor, it is also a great healer. In God's good time humankind will see the wisdom at work behind the problems and shadows of today. When the shadows are darkest, we sometimes forget that God's wisdom is still at work. But when we raise our consciousness above the clouds to view the celestial rainbow, we will know that the sun (Son) is shining and that the Christ life is the only enduring life. That which is not of the Christ must disintegrate because it lacks the love force which holds human life on its divine course. Watch then, and pray, and never let your confidence be shaken. Rather, assist in all ways possible and await the gradual breaking through of divine light in the affairs of the world.

The Music of the Spheres

Do you hear the soft stirring of the musical strains of the song of songs flowing through you? It is a gentle beckoning that stirs your thinking. It is a creative force which is constantly at work in people and in all creation and which opens wide the doors of possibility for you. Love is your personal "go" light, while anything less than a loving nature is a "stop" light! The song of songs is the song of divine love. Love is real. It works! Love is gentle, yet is undoubtedly your strongest tool. You are living and moving right now in this tremendous energy field. From an early Christian manuscript comes a beautiful admonition:

*Nor can that endure which has not its
foundation upon love,*
*For love alone diminishes not, but shines
with its own light;*
*Makes an end of discord, softens the fires
of hate, restores peace in the world,
brings together the sundered,*
*Redresses wrong, aids all and injures
none;*
*And who so invokes its aid will have no
fear of future ill,*
But shall find safety, and have everlasting peace.

What greater depiction of this wondrous Truth is there than that recorded in the "Song of Solomon," or the "Song of Songs" in the Bible? Although often attributed to King Solomon, the authorship of this love poem is unknown. The poem tells the story of three main characters: King Solomon, a Shulamite maiden, and a young shepherd boy whom the maiden loves and who loves her.

The Shulamite maiden has been captured and taken to live in the harem of King Solomon's palace. Although the king woos her ardently, the maiden yearns for her true love, the young shepherd, and she remembers the beauty and trueness of the love they shared. The women of the harem are in awe of the maiden's deep feeling for the one she loves. They marvel that she prefers the simple life of the shepherd to the royal life Solomon offers. In demonstrating the depth and sincerity of her love, she adjures the women not to treat love lightly, for true love is *strong as death.* (Song of Sol. 8:6)

Finally, escaping from the palace, the maiden is reunited with her lover and becomes his bride. The moral of the poem is contained in chapter 8, verse 7: *Many waters cannot quench love, neither can floods drown it. If a man offered for love all the wealth of his house, it would be utterly scorned.*

The mystical overtones contained in this poem are readily apparent. The Shulamite maiden represents the greatest expression of soul integrity and virtue in the depth of her love for the shepherd boy for whom her soul longed. The final uniting of the bride and bridegroom is the wedding of the soul and Spirit, the mystical union which comes out of the soul's longing and seeking for oneness with God.

Yes, this is the song of songs, the love *for* God in which we experience the love *of* God in action within our lives, the divine presence which sings its song of love through every particle of creation. The love you send forth to those who are near and dear to you is but a reminder, a reflection, of that divine mystery in which every human being partakes. Yet, how often we block our own good by forgetting that our thoughts are the molders of our world!

Recognizing the Divine Promise

A story is told of a prince who was kidnapped at birth from his father's palace. Raised in poverty in a poor village, the young prince soon rebelled against the conditions in his life. As he grew into manhood, he carefully constructed a plan for becoming king. Through a series of schemes and battles, he finally won the throne. But he wasn't happy. He was anxious, hostile, and fearful that some other ambitious person could take the throne from him as he had taken it from another. He lived in dread, and his life was miserable.

One day an old beggar arrived at the palace kitchen and told a strange story of a kidnapped prince and alluded to the fact that the kidnapped prince was none other than the present monarch! The beggar was brought before the king and the king learned his true identity—that he was in reality a king by birthright. Immediately he realized the folly of trying to retain by force that which he possessed as a natural inheritance. With his newly gained insight, he began to change and developed a truly kingly consciousness. He had no fear, no feeling of being threatened, only quiet dominion!

You, too, are a child of royal birth. You are an offspring of macrocosmic Mind. Until this Truth becomes a realization in your own consciousness, you will not know yourself enough to trust yourself, to have faith in your many abilities, to be assured of eternal safety, prosperity, peace, and well-being. *The error thought in your mind which causes you to assume you are anything less than the child of a king is the source of every misunderstanding in life that may perplex you!*

Aldous Huxley once remarked: *It is because we don't know who we are, because we are unaware that the Kingdom of Heaven is within us, that we behave in the generally silly, the often insane, the sometimes criminal ways that are so characteristically human. We are saved, we are liberated and enlightened, by perceiving the hitherto unperceived good that is already within us, by returning to our eternal Ground and remaining where, without knowing it, we always have been.*

Certain immutable laws were established in the beginning of creation. These laws are fixed in universal consciousness, and whenever there is no interference or no special application of the universal consciousness, these laws are completely fulfilled.

There is also the creative power of the human mind, which is a part of the universal creative power, and this mind power can affect the elements of the universe by applying other existing universal laws and compelling the elements to obey. How does this work? Let's say that the involved elements are like a large bowling ball. Imagine you are in a bowling alley with a long, smooth bowling lane ahead of you. If you stand at one end of the bowling lane and roll the ball along the floor swiftly and smoothly, it will roll in a straight line to the opposite end of the lane. In taking this action, the ball is following a universal law of cause and effect.

Let's take a closer look. You roll the ball down the bowling lane and the directive force you use propels it in that straight line toward the pins at the opposite end of the lane. Now, if you place an obstacle, like a large brick, on the floor in the middle of the lane and try to roll the ball in a straight line, when the ball strikes the brick, it will be pushed aside and veer from the straight line of previous travel. Thus, the brick becomes an interference in the way of the ball and in the fulfillment of natural law. In putting the brick on the bowling lane, you used your own mind to direct the universal law, or, in other words, to modify its operation!

This same analogy holds true in your thinking. You, as the roller of the ball, can shepherd your thoughts and ascertain that they are positive and good, or you may allow erroneous thinking to cause you to veer from the direct path of accomplishment and fulfillment. Doesn't it make sense that, if you really *know* something, you move forward with greater confidence, greater assurance, and increased capacity to accomplish your desires!

Know and believe the divine promise. You are a child of the living God—the omnipotent, creative Source of all there is. You are born of God. You are truly divine. You have all power, all ability, all capacity to do Godlike things. Psalms 82:6 says: *I say, "You are gods, sons of the Most High, all of you . . . ."*

Think about this. Can you imagine anything greater, more powerful, more dynamic than realizing your own heritage, and then stepping forward to claim it? Is there any wonder that you hear the magnetic calling of the song of songs within the core of your being? Give thanks that the way is wondrously open for bringing forth the radiance of your own Christ self!

The Song of Service

When I was at Unity Village several years ago during a time of tests and interviews to become a minister, someone asked me the question, "Would you be willing to go anywhere in the world where you might be needed, and serve?"

My first reaction was that the unfolding of Truth studies and sharings held such deep meaning that any physical or geographical location would be acceptable. The opportunity to be of service was most important, and I had strong faith in God's divine order to draw me to my true place. Upon returning to my home, the question and the word "service" echoed through my mind. "Service" is a word we use frequently, but do we definitely understand what it means? Some of the Webster dictionary meanings of "service" are: *... the occupation or condition of a servant, employment, a branch or department of employment, work done or duty performed for another such as professional service, repair service; respect, attention, the serving of Truth as through good works, prayer, etc.; any helpful, beneficial or friendly action or conduct, an act giving assistance to another....*

The definitions continue in this vein extensively. So, the idea began to form that service isn't simply some grandiose act or some magnificent obsession. Service isn't limited to those with highly specialized academic degrees, immense fortunes, or great worldly knowledge. Service is something we each can do, can give, and can enjoy every day of our lives.

Who Can Serve and How?

I marvel at the services Jesus Christ performed for humanity. After His overcoming in the wilderness, Jesus, filled with the Spirit, returned to Galilee, where He taught in the synagogues. As we follow the teaching of Jesus and His disciples, a common element flows through all their experiences: the sturdy foundation of faith, worship, and loving service.

As we discover God in our own way and follow the guideposts of the Way-Shower in our own way, in like manner we bring our personal contributions to life. This wide variety of experience adds to the spiritual enrichment of all and helps us all be of service.

God's Spirit Is Creative

During a vacation several years ago at Natural Bridge in Virginia, while walking along a forest trail toward a hidden waterfall, I became intrigued at the large variety of tiny wildflowers that carpeted the forest floor, curtained the massive granite walls, and peeked from underneath rocks and behind shrubs and trees. The woods exhibited a rainbow of color, and every delicate blossom was unique and perfect unto itself. Each flower was a work of art. Gathered as a congregation in their natural habitat, the effect was astonishing and glorious! By being itself, each flower gave its gift of service through the beauty of its being.

Life's activities so often seem *ordinary*. However, when we apply loving service for God in our daily occupations and activities, how tremendously our lives are quickened and enriched. Living each moment to the fullest, we become hospitable and loving in all things.

It is said that some of the finest lace in the world is produced in a small city in Belgium. Each workroom is kept completely dark, except for a small window that admits light directly on the pattern of the lace that is being made! The spinner sits where the narrow shaft of light falls on the thread of his handiwork. The choicest lace is wrought then when the worker himself remains in the dark and only the pattern is in the light.

Using this as an analogy, we can see that to bring forth the loveliest life, the most beautiful design of living, we are to direct our attention and devotion and vision, not to the darkness of personal failures, human limitations, and shadowy appearances of negation, but to the pattern of light which is inherent within the soul of each person. This truly is the design we wish to see develop.

The pattern of light is the resurrection power of the mighty I AM identity, the Christ indwelling every person. Jesus Himself followed this procedure, proclaiming: *"I am the way, and the truth, and the life..."* and, *"I am the resurrection and the life...."* (John 14:6 and John 11:25)

If we follow His example, we, too, earn the right to proclaim that the I AM, the Christ Self within, is the way, the Truth, the resurrection, and the life. Jesus backed His words with action. That action often manifested as service to those who followed to hear Him.

You can become conscious of the life in the words of Jesus given in Mark 10:45 when He said: *"For the Son of man also came not to be served but to serve...."*

In her book, *What Are You?*, Imelda Shanklin states that: *The power in life, in earth, and in heaven lies in the ability to minister or serve, thus, service is coordination with the laws of being.*

Often you cannot measure the work you have accomplished, but it is stamped indelibly on your soul and on the souls of those you have helped come into their own. Thank the loving Father that opportunities are given to you to perform some service every day of your life. Remember that the service you render each day never dies, because in giving this service to others, you are increasing the law of love as well as increasing your own spiritual growth and strength.

The Spirit of the Lord is upon you. Rejoice that you have been brought within the orbit of service, complete with the means, ability, personal gifts, and the power to express the love of God. Rejoice that you wear some of the divine emblems of the Holy Spirit—sincerity, courage, faith, strength, zeal, and a deep desire to serve. Know always that in your life and labor you attract to yourself the power that will help you to continue to serve.

Never forget that the supreme purpose of your life is the unfoldment of Spirit within you. Pay attention to the requirements of your eternal nature. This will bring you a true perspective of your life and the growing knowledge that you are an immortal soul, expressing through a mortal form. Greater strengths and abilities will come to you as you allow the presence and the power of God to work through you.

Spirit is Master, and matter is servant. Spirit is King, and matter is subject. Spirit is God, and you are a part of God. One of the greatest joys of service is to know that from day to day you are fulfilling the purpose of your nature. The power of the Spirit is flowing freely through you, touching souls with whom you come in contact; touching them perhaps for the first time—in some subtle way—but planting a seed thought, enabling them to begin to awaken to wholeness or to become aware of a fresh opportunity to enjoy all that life has to offer.

Whenever this work can be done in any corner of your world, regardless of the size of that corner, light is brought to another soul, and the flame of Truth and love burns a little brighter because of you and your efforts.

Every avenue of service ranks the same with God. There is no first; there is no last. Your true service is that which only you can render. Each of you is an ambassador of Truth and light! Use your precious and special abilities to the fullest measure, and from deep within your real Self will resound the words, "Well done, good and faithful servant."

Now is the time to sing the song of service. Now is the time to help somebody and yourself! Where you are right now is the place to begin. Let the keynote of all thoughts and actions in your life be gentle, loving service. Let the quality of your own life add to the expanding light of God so this light can manifest in all its glory to mankind.

It is often said, "A man must not let himself be ruled by life, but he must direct his own life." This expression has its philosophical value, and more. There is a growing tide of aspiration toward new vision for better ways of life for all people everywhere in the world. Human consciousness is opening to greater spiritual impression and to the realization that there are desirable spiritual values to be built into every aspect of life. These values concern essential attitudes of mind and heart which determine actions and create the circumstances of daily life.

You and I and every child of God can light the way into a better future for mankind as a whole, fulfilling a true "leadership" role through the discipline of self to a more illumined way of living, and through selfless service to all we meet on the journey.

Rainbow Meditation

I AM not lonesome or apart
That you must think, "Lo, there!"
I AM the all emerged in all.
Behold me everywhere, Beloved!
I AM the morning, zephyr soft
While skipping over the lea;
I AM the music of the brook
Flowing ever to the sea.
I AM warm radiant kisses of the sun.
I AM the caressing tears of rain.
I AM the welcome breath of spring
That brings new life again.
I AM the sprouting of the seed,
The budding of a flower.
I AM the beauty that you see
Unfolding every hour.
I AM the joy song of the birds,
The rustling of the leaves;
I AM the holy force of life
In everything that breathes.
I AM the thrill of harmony

You feel but cannot tell;
I AM the firm, unchanging law
That worketh all things well.
I AM the Light that never fails,
The Power that never dies.
I AM the still, small voice within
That bids the soul, "Arise!"
I AM the fruit of highest thought,
I AM the iron rod
That strengthens and supports you;
I AM what men call God.
I AM the soft, sweet murmur
That says your soul belongs
In service to the greatest work.
I AM the song of songs!

Rainbow Promises for Your Personal Needs

"... *call upon me in the day of trouble; I will deliver you, and you shall glorify me.*" (Psalms 50:15)

"*Ask, and it will be given you; seek, and you will find; knock, and it will be opened to you.*" (Matt. 7:7)

"*If you keep my commandments, you will abide in my love, just as I have kept my Father's commandments and abide in his love.*" (John 15:10)

"*This is my commandment, that you love one another as I have loved you.*" (John 15:12)

He who walks in integrity will be delivered, but he who is perverse in his ways will fall into a pit. (Prov. 28:18)

Draw near to God and he will draw near to you. (James 4:8)

... your sins are forgiven .... (I John 2:12)

Call to me and I will answer you, and will tell you great and hidden things which you have not known. (Jer. 33:3)

And this is what he has promised us, eternal life. (I John 2:25)

"... If you continue in my word, you are truly my disciples, and you will know the truth, and the truth will make you free." (John 8:31, 32)

Have no anxiety about anything, but in everything by prayer and supplication with thanksgiving let your requests be made known to God. And the peace of God, which passes all understanding, will keep your hearts and your minds in Christ Jesus. (Phil. 4:6, 7)

Let's Raise Hell!

When Jesus walked upon Earth, people experienced inner conflicts, fears, lack, disease, and death the same as in our modern age. People then also sought here and there for happiness and Truth, as we so often do. Some of them became discouraged and quit the quest. Perhaps they failed to realize, as we sometimes do, that no person can be truly helped until he begins to understand his divine nature.

As spiritual illumination increases, so emerges a deeper understanding of the individual's relationship with God. People often worship God in expressions of outer adoration; but those who are spiritually awakened worship Him in Spirit and in Truth. This involves absolute union with the object of our worship. An understanding of this union seems to be what Jesus was teaching in John 4:7-15:

> *There came a woman of Samaria to*

draw water. Jesus said to her, "Give me a drink." For his disciples had gone away into the city to buy food. The Samaritan woman said to him, "How is it that you, a Jew, ask a drink of me, a woman of Samaria?" For Jews have no dealings with Samaritans. Jesus answered her, "If you knew the gift of God, and who it is that is saying to you, 'Give me a drink,' you would have asked him and he would have given you living water." The woman said to him, "Sir, you have nothing to draw with, and the well is deep; where do you get that living water? Are you greater than our father Jacob, who gave us the well, and drank from it himself, and his sons, and his cattle?" Jesus said to her, "Every one who drinks of this water will thirst again, but whoever drinks of the water that I shall give him will never thirst; the water that I shall give him will become in him a spring of water welling up to eternal life." The woman said to him, "Sir, give me this water, that I may not thirst, nor come here to draw."

This Scripture contains perhaps one of the most important lessons we can absorb, for the Way-Shower is revealing to us the way out of all human limitation and pointing clearly the way to spiritual attainment.

From metaphysical studies we know that each character in this story represents some aspect of our own nature. The Jews depict our spiritual nature. The Samaritans represent our dual, or split, state of consciousness. This is the consciousness that knows of oneness with God, yet, at the same time, entertains a belief in a separation from God. So, in understanding the analogy, we can see why Jesus indicates that salvation emerges from the Jews.

Jesus represents the Christ self of each person. This is the Self He referred to when He mentioned the Father within Him who does the works. The "well" where Jesus met the Samaritan woman is that place within each person where the intellect and the spiritual aspect of being meet. The Samaritan woman shows us the mixed state of consciousness which approaches the well, seeking to draw upon the intellect for assistance. But the Christ self makes contact with her and requests a cooling drink. The woman is greatly astonished at this request, for the Jews (our spiritual nature) will have nothing to do with a mixed state of consciousness.

Jesus was traveling in the Holy Land, which is divided into three sections: Judea, Samaria, and Galilee. Jesus' work began in Judea, expanded into Samaria, and concluded in Galilee where He conducted the major part of His ministry of service. Judea was the center of religious activity for the Jews, and in the Hebrew language means *spirituality, prayer, and praise;* Samaria means *mixed race, mixed states of mind;* and Galilee represents *outer activity or manifestation.* Our own consciousness is represented by these three states in that they show us the steps we take in making our own demonstrations.

Initially we, too, travel into Judea through our attitudes of spirituality, prayer, and praise. Entering into our quiet times we begin to recognize the presence and power of God and absorb what we can from this awareness. Upon arising from these contacts with the Christ within, we move forward into the daily activities of our lives and proceed to make outer demonstrations in accordance with our inner consciousness. But we travel through the Samaritan state of mind.

Here is where we can get confused. Here is

where the mixed state of consciousness plays havoc with our good intentions. We believe that God will answer our sincere prayers, but . . . . We believe . . . and we wonder. Will my prayer really be answered? We believe, and we don't believe. Is there any wonder we fail to get clear answers from a consciousness that is fed such conflicting information? We do persist, however, in our efforts, and finally make it into Galilee.

At last we make our demonstration of conscious union with God and begin to manifest our good. Let's observe an example from daily experiences. Perhaps you have prayed for a healing to take place. After making the call, you wait for the results to become manifest in the Samaritan state of mind. Remember, it was in Samaria that Jesus waited for His disciples to return from purchasing food in the village. While waiting, you talk with the woman at the well, who represents any of us. During the conversation, she expresses the same doubts, fears, hopes, and desires we all voice at some time. She, like each of us, has questions to ask, exhibits an attitude analytical in expression, and has the tendency of the intellect to put up a good argument! When the Master told her that He

would give her living water and she would
never thirst again, she argued with Him saying: *"Sir, you have nothing to draw with, and
the well is deep . . . !"* Does this sound
familiar?

The unillumined intellect can offer so many
reasons why God can't fulfill our needs and
an equal number of reasons why we can't realize our good—if it is allowed to do so. How
many times have you heard expressions such
as, "I want to be healthy, but . . . "; "I want
to get a good job, but . . . "; "I want to grow
spiritually, but I'm only human"; "I want to
give, but with the economy the way it is . . ."?
And on and on we give excuses, while the well
gets deeper and the doubts increase!

Every one of us stands in the presence of
the Christ, even as did the woman of Samaria. His activity is ready to spring up within us as the living waters that bring the fulfillment of every need. Yet, when we live in a
mixed state of consciousness, we live in a
veritable hell! We express, like the Samaritan
woman, "I see absolutely no way whereby my
immediate needs can be met. Oh, woe is me!"

No, it isn't simple to raise a hellish consciousness to a higher state. The long years—
perhaps lifetimes—spent in negative atti-

tudes and emotions are a mire through which
we must move. Christhood isn't achieved in a
single step! Like Peter, we may cry out numerous times, "Lord, save me or I perish!"

You cannot control anything in your world
as long as you are controlled by it. And the
fact that you try, seem to fail, and still seek
God is an indication that you are progressing.
The only God you can ever know is the God of
your own inner life, and the only place you
can contact that God is within yourself. Turn
your attention to the indwelling Christ and
keep it there!

1. *Regardless of your need, know there
   is an answer.* It is certainly acceptable to realize you have a need in life
   and believe that, with God as your
   teammate, the right answer will be revealed, and at the proper time.

2. *Don't try to tell God how to do His
   work.* He knows the depth of the well.
   The entire universe is His to know
   and to utilize—past, present, future,
   seen and unseen, finite and infinite.
   Nothing that will serve the purpose of
   assisting you to acquire a spiritual
   consciousness is overlooked.

3. *Ask for assistance from your Christ*

self. You don't have to bear any burden alone. Although a part of you may raise questions and doubts, continue to reach in faith to learn the higher and better way.

Jesus taught that the kingdom of God is within you. Well, if the kingdom is there, so is the King! It is that omnipresent Spirit manifesting itself to and through you. Think of this marvelous Spirit as the Father/Creator of your being, eternally connected with you. You are a channel for its expression. Truly, you live, move, and have your being in this Spirit!

Whatever your life situation today may be, embark on the journey into Judea, giving praise and thanksgiving for the wonderful presence of God moving through you. Continue into and through Samaria, giving little thought to any semblance of confusion, doubt, or untruth. The day will come when you arrive in the Galilee expression of consciousness and your demonstration of your realization of conscious union with God is assured!

Mighty Drops of Water!

The following ideas are offered as food for thought in planning your day. Each expression can be a drop of the "living water" if you use the essence of Truth contained therein.

The greatest sin is *fear.*

The best day of your life is *today.*

The most agreeable companion is *one who would receive you as you are.*

The greatest deceiver is *one who deceives himself.*

The greatest production secret is *eliminate wasted effort; be concise.*

The best recreation is *soul work.*

The greatest comfort is the *knowledge that you did your work well.*

The greatest mistake is *giving up.*

The most expensive indulgence is *hate.* (Hate takes its toll in all aspects of your being!)

The cheapest, easiest, and most destructive thing is *finding fault.*

The greatest stumbling block is an *inflated ego.*

The most severe bankruptcy is the *soul that has lost enthusiasm.*

The most clever person is *one who fol-*

lows the inner guidance.

The most dangerous person is the *liar.*

The greatest need is *common sense.*

The greatest puzzle is *life,* but it can be solved!

The greatest thought is *God.*

The greatest thing in the world is *love.*

The truest solace is *prayer.*

The greatest inspiration is a *divine idea whose time has come.*

The most glorious miracle is *you!*

Removing the "Thorn in the Flesh"

Many of us have read of Paul's thorn in the flesh mentioned in II Corinthians 12:7-9. Paul says: *And to keep me from being too elated by the abundance of revelations, a thorn was given me in the flesh, a messenger of Satan, [the Adversary, contradictor, liar in wait], to harass me, to keep me from being too elated. Three times I besought the Lord about this, that it should leave me; but he said to me, "My grace is sufficient for you, for my power is made perfect in weakness." I will all the more gladly boast of my weaknesses, that the power of Christ may rest upon me.*

This particular episode in Paul's life has

baffled many persons. I've even heard some say, "Shouldn't I glory in my weakness as did Paul?" Well, we know the reply to that statement. As students of Truth, we know there is a meaningful answer, one that is satisfying in accordance with the nature of God.

What, then, is the explanation of Paul's thorn in the flesh? The clue seems to lie in II Corinthians: 11:24-28, where Paul lists his many persecutions. He says:

Five times have I received at the hands of the Jews the forty lashes less one. Three times I have been beaten with rods; once I was stoned. Three times I have been shipwrecked; a night and a day I have been adrift at sea; on frequent journeys, in danger from rivers, danger from robbers, danger from my own people, danger from Gentiles, danger in the city, danger in the wilderness, danger at sea, danger from false brethren; in toil and hardship, through many a sleepless night, in hunger and thirst, often without food, in cold and exposure. And, apart from other things, there is the daily pressure upon me of my anxiety for all the churches.

Paul refers to his persecutions as "messengers" of Satan, which is the same explanation he applies in chapter twelve when referring to his thorn in the flesh. Paul was a learned man who was well-schooled in the Hebrew Scriptures of the Old Testament, where trials and sufferings inflicted by others are often described as thorns.

In Truth, we understand that unhappy experiences of any kind, which may seem negative while happening, are really good opportunities for spiritual growth in disguise. From this perspective, Paul's thorns in the flesh are not necessarily physical infirmity, rather, likely the many sufferings he experienced through the actions of others.

In His Sermon on the Mount, Jesus placed suffering by persecution in a different category from illness and disease. He stated: *"Blessed are those who are persecuted for righteousness' sake, for theirs is the kingdom of heaven."* (Matt. 5:10) Who among us has not, at some time in our lives, experienced the heavy weight of some burden or sorrow. We recognize that such experience comes about as a result of error thinking or distorted mental attitudes sent forth as cause at some time in our past. We name our own affliction because it is peculiar to us, and we experience the effect as an opportunity for personal overcoming. Paul, himself, sowed some pretty severe seeds of persecution toward others, and we know that, as a man sows, so shall he reap.

The Beatitude mentioned earlier promises that those who are persecuted for the sake of righteousness shall experience the kingdom of heaven, which means that a new consciousness emerges—the Christ consciousness. As we increasingly abide in this "heavenly" rather than "hellish" state of consciousness, we no longer suffer what Shakespeare called *the slings and arrows of outrageous fortune.* We no longer suffer because we no longer take offense at the offerings of life, realizing that we alone are the sowers and the reapers. Upon reaching this understanding and awareness, we become truly spiritually non-resistant through overcoming that which may be termed negative by the truth we know and express.

It is our involvement with things personal that plants the thorns in the flesh and provides them with the nourishment to flourish in our consciousness. The real you is a loving, joyous being who is truthful and honest. No matter what mistakes you may have made, you are good and you are wonderful.

Paul said that he died daily, meaning, I'm certain, that we die to the limiting personal aspects of our nature. Jesus also said that in order to keep our lives, we must lose them. It is important to be willing to let go of the personal, small self and all its preoccupations with restrictive circumstances such as prejudices, resentments, and aloofness. We lose not one thing that is important when we surrender the personal self and align our will with the will of God. Rather, we gain more than can be expressed in mere words. All that is worthwhile for spiritual growth, plus divine dividends of peace of mind and assurance that we are not alone, are showers of blessings unlimited.

We place our footsteps more firmly along the path of evolving consciousness and walk triumphant, without those thorns that prick at us when we walk in the flesh instead of in the Spirit.

The Price of Christ Consciousness

All life's occurrences, again, are for the purpose of training the student. If you do not profit from them, you are selling yourself short. It isn't logical to expect everything to always go according to personal will. You may not yet know all of your divine plan. So dream the dream of spiritual evolution, which is more wonderful than you presently conceive.

Seek not spiritual unfoldment with selfish motives, but rather with the desire that, through your ability to become healthy, prosperous, and wise, you may more effectively assist your fellow travelers. You are now placed in the life position where your efforts and your love and your development are most needed. Some work before the public. Some labor quietly. Always you are—and will be— where you possess opportunities of doing the greatest good for yourself and for humanity. Whether or not your name becomes well-known and you attain to great heights of fame is unimportant.

The whole purpose of spiritual development is designed for the individual to so train himself that he can become a more powerful center of light from which God light and love may radiate. We've mentioned this reality already. Be prepared to pay the price of spiritual development and undergo the training required to elevate your consciousness. Such training requires continually working on your mental outlook. Strive to live a life of wholeness, kindness, peacefulness. Refuse to be overshadowed or obsessed by fear, anger, or any other human desire or passion. Exhibitions of these emotions indicate the mind is undisciplined, inharmonious, and dis-eased. A healthy mind is an unparalleled receiving as well as broadcasting station. Develop within yourself that which you desire to attain. Begin now. And especially be at peace with all you meet, and remain harmonious in all your endeavors.

You are human. You are also fundamentally divine. A firm determination that the divinity within shall shine forth, and so transform your life and circumstances, brings the desired result. Once you contact and hold fast to the source of stillness and peace within you, the tone of your whole being becomes elevated. Pray unceasingly that you may be kindled with the magic light of hope, so you will press onward, growing in spiritual knowledge and becoming more aware of eternal Truth. As you advance increasingly in harmony with God, and with love, your needs will be supplied in the natural course of your daily living.

Stop to consider that giving and receiving are two halves of the same whole. You are equally responsible for both. Strive for balance in all you do. As you overcome your desires—as the lower self is conquered—as you use every life experience as a stepping-stone to your Christ self, so do you progress, rung by rung, up the ladder of regeneration. You have the capacity to climb *within* as you will. You are a potential master on the path. Know that it is the purified heart, not the intellectual head, which leads to the Master's feet.

More Truth About You

God took the real you—the Spirit—and clothed it with mind and body. You received the gift of free will so you would have a mind free to think *as you direct it.* As mentioned earlier, it is the misdirection of your mind that causes problems. Likewise, it is the right use of your mind that solves these problems. Your mind is an avenue of awareness, an instrument, through which you can recognize and acknowledge what is. Decide what you want and start working in that direction. The power within you is greater than you, but only you can determine its use.

Wherever one's consciousness flows, it retains the stamp of its identity pattern; and all that it breathes in of the universal essence of God's consciousness coalesces around that pattern to widen the borders of one's individuality. As we expand in consciousness, God expands His infinite awareness of Himself through us. Therefore, learn to stand within the citadel of being, insulated by the mighty currents of the Holy Spirit. You are then capable of reaching out in deepest mercy and love with a response to all, which is indicated by your inner God nature.

> *I stood in a fragrant meadow and looked*
> *toward a hill.*
> *There, I beheld men and women and*
> *children*
> *Standing with their hands joined in*
> *fellowship.*
> *Each one looked into the eyes of the*
> *other,*
> *And no one was afraid.*
> *I asked the angel by my side, "What*
> *place is this?"*
> *Smiling, the angel replied, "This is*
> *Heaven."*

*I asked the angel, "Pray tell, where is
this place?"*
*The angel answered, "In the conscious-
ness of your heart."*
*I thought for a while, observing the
serenity about me.*
*Next, I asked the angel, "When does this
happen?"*
*And the angel said, "When all men and
women and children*
*learn to love one another as God has ever
loved you!"*

Rainbow Meditation

Father-Mother God, in whom I truly live and move and have my being, I now understand and know that loving You opens wide the windows of my soul, through mind in expression, to the eternal verities of life.

Therefore, I will be true to the great mission whereunto I am called. I seek to manifest Thy glory in myself. I come humbly into this arena of human service, joyfully do that which needs to be done by me, and go out not until I have completed the mission set before me.

As I love You, the Lord, my God, I open my heart for forgiveness and compassion for myself and others. Thus my consciousness is cleansed and ready to receive more of the good You have for me.

I open my consciousness to the unity of all life, releasing mighty channels for Your light and love to bring increased blessings to mankind.

My soul is clothed with high ideals, set in the midst of new opportunities, and can hear the angels of love singing, "Come to the great Indwelling and know perfect peace."

Thank You, God, for guiding me along the paths of righteousness, in the right use of the power and authority you have invested in me and in all your children. Through this power and authority, I am poised and prepared in all situations and circumstances.

Knowing that heaven and Earth come together in the one who is grateful,

> *In Thy life, I live.*
> *In Thy love, I express.*
> *In Thy light, I see clearly.*
> *In Thy Truth, I joyously share.*
> *Forever!*

Your Exodus!

A story is told of a man who lay dying in a European hospital. After extensive examination, the physicians told the man they were unable to diagnose his ailment and, until they were successful in pinpointing the problem, there was no way they could treat him. If the physicians could determine what the problem was, they felt certain the right medicine could be prescribed. There was one possibility, however, they told the patient. A great and famous physician from Vienna was scheduled to visit the hospital soon. Perhaps he would be able to make a diagnosis. The patient was filled with hope at this positive news and eagerly awaited the arrival day of the honored physician.

Finally the great doctor came. Local physicians trailed along behind him as he made his way from room to room, observing the various patients and diagnosing their illnesses. When he passed the bed of the patient in our story, he paused, looked down at the medical record chart, gave a fleeting glance at the patient, and murmured one word, "Moribundus!" The patient was overjoyed! To his understanding, he had a simple disease which was diagnosed in seconds by the learned physician, and he proceeded to get well! No one told him that "moribundus" is the Latin word which means "to die"!

What happened? Actually, it's simple. We know that the life urge is always stronger than the death urge in anyone; and in this particular case, the famous physician's negative pronouncement over the patient had no effect whatsoever over the powerful life urge of the man who was ill! If the patient had *understood* the language spoken, and *believed* what was said, he might have promptly expired! Instead, the life urge within him was so strong that with what he thought was encouragement, he was healed, even though his belief came about through a misunderstanding. The man was able to make a personal exodus from sickness into a health-filled life.

Perhaps you, too, have experienced times in your life when you became dissatisfied with yourself or the unsatisfying things you were experiencing. From deep within, you felt a positive urge to get up and take charge of your life through positive action, to change things for the better.

If you have ever felt like this, I believe a closer look at the Rainbow Promise found in Exodus 14:10-14, will help you to understand yourself a little better with regard to how you function and how you can move forward in your life in spite of seeming negative influences.

When Pharoah drew near, the people of Israel lifted up their eyes, and behold, the Egyptians were marching after them; and they were in great fear. And the people of Israel cried out to the Lord; and they said to Moses, "Is it because there are no graves in Egypt that you have taken us away to die in the wilderness? What have you done to us, in bringing us out of Egypt? Is not this what we said to you in Egypt, 'Let us alone and let us serve the Egyptians'? For it would have been better for us to serve the Egyptians than to die in the wilderness." And Moses said to the people, "Fear not, stand firm, and see the salvation of the Lord, which he will work for you today;

for the Egyptians whom you see today,
you shall never see again. The Lord will
fight for you, and you have only to be
still. "

In this Scripture, we see the children of
Israel coming out of their long bondage in
Egypt. They are making a great exodus. And
that exodus is happening today. *Every one of*
us, as we make this earth journey, is making
an exodus.

Exodus means getting out of trouble or being released from limitation. This Scripture
lesson is descriptive of the human soul, or
consciousness, growing and evolving out of
the sense part of man into spiritual enlightenment. Lodged in the human consciousness
are many conditions of thought and feeling
that would be best left unmanifested! How
fortunate for us that there is a glorious power
in Truth and the Holy Spirit that can be used
to erase all undesirable patterns of imperfec-
tion from the screens of mind and heart and
guide us out of the exodus of human bondage.
Wise are the souls who avail themselves of
every opportunity to make forward progress
through the right use of thoughts, feelings,
and actions. Wise are those who amplify their
ideals as well as their vision of the standard

of universal perfection and make it an active guiding principle in life.

Moses was inspired to visit the Pharoah and plead with him to let the children of Israel go free. After many bitter experiences, the Pharoah finally released the people, and Moses began the long journey of leading the people out of bondage toward the Promised Land. However, like many who are restricted in their personal bondages, the people proceeded reluctantly, not at all sure they wanted to follow along and become free! The children of Israel placed most of the responsibility of the journey on Moses, and when trouble or hardships came along, they were quick to cry out and blame Moses! *When someone is helping us try to break free of a situation, we, too, may be quick to blame him if some unforeseen difficulty emerges—unless we abide in an illumined consciousness.*

As the children of Israel fled on their journey and the Pharoah gave pursuit, they panicked into utter helplessness. They growled at Moses for bringing them to their present point. But Moses quickly and confidently declared: *"Fear not, stand firm, and see the salvation of the Lord, which he will work for you today. . . . The Lord will fight for you, and you have only to be still.''*

I wonder how Moses felt later when he cried to God for help and was answered, *"Why do you cry to me? Tell the people of Israel to go forward. Lift up your rod, and stretch out your hand over the sea and divide it, that the people of Israel may go on dry ground through the sea. And I will harden the hearts of the Egyptians so that they shall go in after them, and I will get glory over Pharoah and all his host, his chariots, and his horsemen. And the Egyptians shall know that I am the Lord . . . .* (Exod. 14:15-18) Regardless of his personal feelings, Moses did as he was instructed by the Lord, and the Red Sea parted, and the children of Israel were led across into safety.

Now, let's relate this story to the present time and to ourselves and the people about us. What do you see exemplified?

This is the story of the conflict of the soul as we develop and grow spiritually.

Each of us have personal times of conflict but, like Moses, we have the ability to meet them and proceed victoriously through them. As Moses turned the Red Sea into a pathway of improvement, so can we!

Metaphysically, Moses represents that in

us which is the *drawing out process of the soul, the progressive evolutionary phase of the soul.* It is the great inner urging within us that constantly beckons us onward. There is also a Pharoah, King of Egypt, aspect of self. It is the intellect which is unwisely used. Egypt within us is that part of the subconscious that is yet unawakened to Truth. It is the land of darkness and ignorance over which Pharoah rules. To assist him, he has an army of thoughts and beliefs which look only to appearances, to the past, to the actions of others, or to the negative side of things, clutching them closely, failing to let them go!

Wherever we may be on our personal path of progression, we still have some Moses and Pharoah in us. We all have thoughts (people) still in bondage, holding us in limitation. It is easy for Pharoah to influence these people, for he says, "Leave things as they are. Why upset the apple cart? It's too much labor to try to improve the world or your situation in life!" And so often people agree with him and become more deeply enmeshed in the vicious circle of bondage.

This is the time to remember that there is a power at work in us that will direct us out of limitation. *We are children of God! We are not meant to serve in bondage!* We do, how-ever, serve in bondage as long as we accept limitation for ourselves or others, put up with it in any manner, or do nothing about it when we can observe its effects.

Now is the time to remember we have a power expressing within us that is greater than any experience or situation. As Moses was instructed to stretch out his rod and part the Red Sea, we can stretch forth the power of the I AM, God's law of right action, the action of all good. The Red Sea can represent any problem or experience we may be going through; but in this instance, it represents the sea of universal thought which is all around us. The Red Sea is composed of all the thoughts and beliefs of mankind that have impregnated the universal ether. They are the mental meanderings of the human mind which must be overcome by the progressive soul.

This sort of striving can be difficult. As Truth students we have left Egypt but are still making our way to the Promised Land. We must follow the advice given to Moses when he was told to *fear not* and *stand still* and *see.* We are not alone. God is with us. As we become still and get attuned with God and with life, we are able to look beyond the appearance of any experience and perceive infinite possibilities.

Now is the time to step out on faith. *"Tell the people of Israel to go forward."* Although Moses and his people could perceive the way across the Red Sea, they still had to place one foot ahead of the other and move forward on the promise. Moses' spiritual growth advances in a slow and orderly manner. So it is for each person. No one can jump into immediate spiritual illumination. For one thing, the spiritual vibrations would destroy the physical body and the working vehicle would be lost. As the bud of the rose must unfold naturally if its majestic full-blown beauty is to be beheld, so do we, too, blossom into the radiance of true beingness.

When you come to a Red Sea place in your life, where regardless of what you do there seems to be no way out, remember, there is also no way back! The only way open is forward. Keep on.

Like the man in the European hospital, as you make your exodus, "Fear not, stand still, and see!" Give thanks that God is guiding you, and each crossing (overcoming of negative thoughts and beliefs) brings you ever closer to the Promised Land.

Exodus-Producing Attitudes

You think you know yourself quite well. In certain areas this may be correct. Residing within your subconscious library is a record of all you have done and all that has happened to you since you were born. You have tremendous capacities, far greater than you suspect. You have learned many skills. Perhaps you are trained in certain areas so you may contribute to the general economy of humanity. Now, expend important energy and learn the most meaningful skills of your life—how to unfold your divine plan!

You are dual in nature, a physical and material body occupied and energized by a spiritual essence. You, as a human being, use two kinds of energy—physical energy and soul (cosmic) energy. Your physical energy comes to you from what you eat and drink and the air you breathe. A small part of your cosmic energy comes in this way, but most of it comes through spiritual attunement with the life-force. This life-force can be likened to transformers which tap the sea of energy around you and condition it for your use.

Physical matter is composed of atoms which, in turn, are composed of electrons, protons, and neutrons, all in perpetual motion. They are particles of energy moving at high speeds. When this cosmic energy is stepped down to a point where it is used by the physical body, it manifests itself very much like electrical energy, only more subtly. Like electricity, it has polarity, and this polarity can be controlled and directed.

What I am saying is: *you are the master of your life*. What you do with the powerful energy within you is your choice. Your attitude is important. So clean house! Get out of the habit of worrying over the little pinpricks of life. Only the sword stabs require attention! Every atom of your being throbs with active intelligence. The very air you breathe and the world in which you live are alive with divine intelligence which seeks to impart to you all you wish to know about everything!

Here are some "idea prompters" which will assist you in making your exodus!

1. *Release all thoughts of self-condemnation!* Remember who and what you are. It's often easy to stop criticizing others, but what about yourself! Self-

condemnation is equally destructive. It saps your wonderful energy and dissipates creative abilities.

2. *Go forth not in arrogance!* Spiritual arrogance is one of the most dangerous forms taken by the ego. Be careful. No one knows so much that he has no room left for additional knowledge. Guard your ego and realize: *It is not I, but the Father who dwells within me who does the work.* You do your part. But lose self in service to others, and self prospers!

3. *Raise your consciousness to an attitude of freedom in Truth!* Faith is the heart of an exodus-producing attitude. Most people recognize the existence of the creative Source, and you can see this wondrous power lovingly at work in the human creation, rejuvenating, changing, restoring, releasing, and glorifying every atom, cell, and electron of your being. And what can stop that?

4. *Keep ever before your vision the divine ideal—the divine blueprint— for humankind!* Be cheerful! Be joyous! Be sincere! A long face isn't the

mark of one seeking to express freedom of Spirit, soul, and body!

The absolute law of every mental or physical manifestation is a culminating externalization of something that previously has occurred within. The outer is the end of the road. Let's work on the inner and the results will certainly be better.

The Wasted Years Returned!

Have you ever made the statement, "I wish I could do such and such over"? When we find ourselves at a certain point of maturity, perhaps we may look back and feel we have wasted time, energy, or opportunity. We may even feel failure. Every person, however, is a living story with many chapters. Each chapter is a dialogue with life of the many experiences we have before we arrive at our spiritual destination.

A Bible story vividly illustrates this point. In the first two chapters of the Book of Joel, the country is ravaged by a swarm of locusts which the prophet regards as heralding the "day of the Lord." Early Bible commentators regarded the locust swarm as merely symbolic imagery, set out with poetic hyperbole.

But modern scholars have caught up with the facts of nature and indicated that it is also a realistic picture.

Vast swarms of these insects (sometimes covering hundreds of square miles) occasionally emerge from their desert breeding grounds in Africa, the Middle East, and parts of Asia and lay waste to a whole countryside in a matter of hours. Anyone who has witnessed this terrifying scourge will recognize in Joel's account a documentary record of unequalled precision and literary power.

The great cloud of locusts darkening the sun and the stars, the noise of the whirring wings and chomping jaws, the fertile landscape turned into a bleached and burned-up wasteland provide startling realism.

In chapter 2, verse 13, the Lord is saying: "*... rend your hearts and not your garments.*" And Joel continues: "*Return to the Lord, your God, for he is gracious and merciful, slow to anger, and abounding in steadfast love .... *"

To "rend your heart" means to repent. In other words, turn from a belief in outer appearances to a belief in God and that which is right. A reversal of mind and heart takes place toward the direction of the All-Good.

Look at your life for a moment. Can you think of a time, or times, when you were in a situation that you would describe as a "time when the locusts have eaten"? This could be a time when you felt no joy in living, no happiness in your world, and no inner peace. There may even have been events of which you are now ashamed, years you would like to forget. Yet, we can't forget these years, for they are a part of our consciousness. But, they can be restored in heart and mind to their rightful place. Memories of those times can be transmuted to represent years of good, years of growth and experience, and not years of evil.

The admonition of Scripture is to *rend your hearts and not your garments*. Garments in this instance represent the outer circumstances of life, while Joel, metaphysically, speaks of *the I AM or Christ in dominion in the individual*. Joel is the *worshiper of God; he who desires; he who wills; he who fulfills every desire*. (Metaphysical Bible Dictionary) And Joel says: "*I will restore to you the years which the swarming locust has eaten.... You shall eat in plenty and be satisfied, and praise the name of the Lord your God, who has dealt wondrously with you.*" (Joel 2:25, 26)

Sometimes we may tend to run from severe experiences. Sometimes we may act oblivious, as if they never happened. Sometimes we may try to cover up inadequacies or errors. And none of these excuses work! The years the locusts have eaten may be a time when trouble reigned in mind and body or other conditions. They could be a time when you almost believed that you were all alone and cruel fate stalked your path, a fate over which you may have felt you had no more control than the helpless farmer whose crops were destroyed by the swarm of locusts. Or, those locust years could be the years when you felt spiritually depleted, or that your prayers were unanswered, or your prosperity consciousness lay at the bottom of the barrel!

Have you thought about the fact that if you didn't have "wasted years," there would be nothing to be returned? *By the very fact that you are here, you are in the business of restoration!* You wouldn't be the person you presently are, you wouldn't be ready for what God has in store for you now, if you had not experienced the activity or the time you may now condemn.

Emerson said: *The past is for us, but the sole terms on which it becomes ours are its subordination to the present.* If you can look back and see what may be termed "wasted years," then there is something you can do. Those years can be restored and made beautiful again. If you restore a house or a painting, you return it to its original beauty and perfection.

You may think you sold your birthright by some past action and are unable to redeem it. But remember, the past is a process of unfoldment—if you allow it to be. Place your past life in its proper light. Put away anxiety and, as mentioned before, self-condemnation, as an adult would put away childish toys.

It doesn't matter what the past has been or what you believe or think about it. Today, it is being restored as part of God unfolding in and through you. *Nothing that has happened in the past can ever separate you from God.* It is never too late to be released. It is never too late to be healed. It is never too late to forgive and be forgiven—by yourself! It is never too late to grow; and it is never too late to begin again!

Restore the past unto the Creator. The outer fullness in life comes quickly when love provides the inner sense of completeness. After you repent—restore your oneness in thought with God—the Holy Spirit pours out abundant blessings. Joel tells us in chapter 2, verse 28, what happens when man is purified: *"And it shall come to pass afterward, that I will pour out my spirit on all flesh; your sons and your daughters shall prophesy, your old men shall dream dreams, and your young men shall see visions."*

Flesh is your manifest being; your sons and daughters are your thoughts and feelings; your old men are the already attained states of consciousness; and your young men are the goals you are presently working toward for fulfillment. And here comes another promise! *"And it shall come to pass that all who call upon the name of the Lord shall be delivered."* (Joel 2:32)

Get Your Engine Running!

A frustrated young man had worked long and hard at building an engine. He tried persistently to get it to run. Nothing happened. In describing his situation to an engineer friend, the young man was told that the construction of an operable engine depends on certain mechanical principles. So, at some point, the builder must have ignored or violated one or more of these principles. The engineer assured the young man that if he would correct his mistakes, the engine would run as intended.

In the mental realm each person exercises complete freedom and authority. With regard to your thoughts you may say to this one, "Go!" and it goes. You may say to another, "Come!" and it comes. Jesus taught us to seek only that which is good and to begin to use our God-given energy to build our understanding of righteousness and Truth. You are never obligated to accept any idea of limitation.

The higher you look, the farther you can see. When you look at the ground with downcast eyes, you can only see a few feet. When you look straight ahead, your scope of vision expands and you can sometimes see the sun, the moon, and the stars millions of miles away! When you realize the wonders of the Christ perfection and the joyous awareness of being a child of God, you are then able to realize that the cares and concerns of life are truly stepping-stones toward greater expression of God in you and, therefore, can be easily solved by using spiritual laws.

As a beloved child of God, you need never

surrender your spiritual authority and dominion because of any negative barrier that may be placed across your path. Like the children of Israel, an exodus awaits you. Lift your eyes above limitation and get into the consciousness of God as love, life, intelligence, substance, and harmony, and proclaim for yourself: *I have the spirit of Truth within. I know it and I show it!*

Rainbow Meditation

Dear God!
How good I feel as I quiet my mind and heart
And seek within for Your inspiration.
I know that Your way is the straight and
*   certain*
Way of accomplishing my goals and realizing
*   my desires.*
In this understanding,
And with a feeling of trust and attunement,
Father/Mother God, I listen to Your voice.
Unfailingly, You reveal to me in calm
*   moments*
Of prayer and meditation
All that which is for my highest good.
I am led out of the valley of ignorance and
*   despair.*
I feel Your presence ever near in the silence.
I make decisions quickly and correctly as I
*   am illumined*
By the light of Your inspiration within me.
The wasted years are returned in radiant

splendor.
That splendor is the initial contact with the
    guiding light
Of Truth as life brings each new and glorious
    experience.
You are in charge of my life.
You lead me in the path of righteousness.
I praise and give thanks for the light
That makes the rough places plain.
I gain a deeper sense of appreciation for all
    my good
As I travel onward, step by step,
Toward the Promised Land.

Parables of Prosperity

*A*n important matter drawn to the attention of people in all walks of life, in all countries in the world, and on all levels of consciousness, is that of supply. Often the question is asked, "How shall I be able to meet the requirements of the day?" These requirements may be physical, mental, emotional, material, or spiritual. Great inner strength is required to live successfully in a world which demands so much from us.

Wouldn't it be wonderful and satisfying to know that your total prosperity is founded upon the solid rock of universal laws and remains unshakable regardless of what storms of adversity may try to disturb you? *This knowing comes from the thoughts you hold in mind.* Negative thoughts are like ants. A single ant may annoy you, but you can easily brush it off and it does you no harm. But let yourself fall asleep on an anthill, and there a thousand ants have the opportunity to swarm over you, and you will certainly wish you had been more careful.

We now stand on the verge of a new state of awareness in matters of prosperity. The first step in moving forward is to realize: *All things whatsoever the Father has are mine.* The promise of Scripture in Deuteronomy 28:11, 12 is: *"And the Lord will make you abound in prosperity .... The Lord will open to you his good treasury."*

The knowing that your prosperity is based on spiritual principles can come through your personal understanding of the parables of prosperity as taught by the Master Jesus. Herein is found the meaning of real and lasting abundance. Within these parables are shown the rules and guidelines required to build a solid prosperity consciousness.

Of course, prosperity isn't the only topic enlightened by these parables. Each story also carries an obvious moral application. In addition, the parables illustrate basic Truth principles of God which are applicable in every phase of life.

Clearly, the person who *hears* and *acts* upon the teachings given by Jesus is like the man who built his house upon the rock. Here is the promise of the fulfillment of your desire for prosperity—that it be founded upon the rock of spiritual Truth. Conversely, prosperity founded upon sand is the result of not *hearing* and *heeding* that which has been proven to be valid.

Let's look at some of these little stories and begin with the parable of the two buildings. The parable is found in Matthew 7:24-27.

"Every one then who hears these words of mine and does them will be like a wise man who built his house upon the rock; and the rain fell, and the floods came, and the winds blew and beat upon that house, but it did not fall, because it has been founded on the rock. And every one who hears these words of mine and does not do them will be like a foolish man who built his house upon the sand; and the rain fell, and the floods came, and the winds blew and beat against that house, and it fell; and great was the fall of it."

The obvious conclusion to draw from this parable is that *prosperity must begin with a firm basis or foundation.* The question, then, is what is this symbol that carries such a strong meaning of security? Upon what basis can we build to be able to withstand any storm? The answer must be to *recognize God as the source of our supply and prosperity in every manifestation.* Your job is not the source of your supply. No person or organization is the source of your supply. No financial investment, no stocks or bonds, no property accumulations can fulfill all your needs. All these aspects of your life have an important function—that of being a meaningful channel through which God's good can flow. But they are not the Source. God is the Source. God is the All-Good. Therefore, every good and beautiful thing that flows into your life must have its beginning in God, and here alone you find the Giver of the good and the Good itself!

Many people who experience an insufficiency of something in life do so because they believe in lack instead of abundance. Folks who believe in this manner are failing to realize that the true source of all abundance is within them; and this nonrealization is a large block preventing the prosperity flow from reaching them. People who see only the channel and not the Source are believing in lack!

We may recognize one or many channels, but there is only one Source. Channels may appear, disappear, expand, contract, and come in all shapes, sizes, and arrangements. It is important to remember that, regardless of what happens to any channel, your good is still available to you. If you believe this and have faith in the promise of God, know that God is your true Source, and stand firm in this knowing, regardless of outer appearances, your prosperity will be constant and sure!

This may mean there is a necessity to narrow your vision to see only God the Good at work in your life. It may mean you have to remove your attention from the multitudinous distractions clamoring for your attention from the appearance world. Look within. Seek the guidance from the Secret Place of the Most High. And this brings us to our next prosperity parable:

"Enter by the narrow gate; for the gate is wide and the way is easy, that leads to destruction, and those who enter by it are many. For the gate is narrow and the way is hard, that leads to life, and those who find it are few." (Matt. 7:13, 14)

It may seem like a paradox to understand that one must narrow the vision in order to observe the good of all of life everywhere. But it's true. When you keep your eye single, seeing only the good, then only the goodness of God fills your sight. We are always as close to success and fulfillment as we are to God's presence in us. When we turn our lives over to God without reservation He can and will do remarkable things through us. *Acknowledge* the presence of God within you. *Practice* the presence of God within you. Let the presence of God *express* through your consciousness as the fulfillment of every need.

Single-eyed Vision of Prosperity

Perhaps one of the most startling secrets about prosperity is the Truth that the door lies right within yourself. Once you recognize this, you have found the master key that can open all other doors to increased abundance.

1. *Prosperity is closer than you think. In fact, it is what you think!*
   What you can conceive, you can achieve. Your world is affected by your thoughts and feelings to a greater degree than you may presently realize.

2. *A basic prosperity law states: Give and you will receive!*
   We know that nature abhors a

vacuum and rushes to fill it. Give of yourself, your time, your energy, your money, and your material possessions. Create the vacuum and open the amazing channels of prosperity to an omnipresent flow into your life.

3. *Align a perfect union between your mind and God Mind.*

   Go to the place within yourself where the will of God is known. The point of contact is seeking and willingness on your part. The ways of superconscious Mind, conscious mind, and subconscious mind are miraculous. Herein is the power to multiply tenfold, fiftyfold, one hundredfold, one thousandfold your heartfelt desires. This is the marvelous law of increase.

4. *Keep your desires to yourself!*

   The reason for this is cosmic. There is absolutely no need to dissipate all the tremendous energy you've generated for your prosperity demonstration (through keeping your eye single) by telling everyone. Your words have power. Once you focus your thoughts and feelings on absolute potential and the energy begins flowing, your sub-conscious mind believes you finally mean business about prosperity. Don't negate this precious effort by pouring your energy helter-skelter upon all who will listen.

The "Chop-Chop" Parable!

I love the idea presented in the following Scripture:

"Beware of false prophets, who come to you in sheep's clothing but inwardly are ravenous wolves. You will know them by their fruits. Are grapes gathered from thorns, or figs from thistles? So, every sound tree bears good fruit, but the bad tree bears evil fruit. A sound tree cannot bear evil fruit, nor can a bad tree bear good fruit. Every tree that does not bear good fruit is cut down and thrown into the fire. Thus you will know them by their fruits." (Matt. 7:15-20)

Remember that only you can set any kind of limit on yourself. Stop saying that you've had a hard time in life. Stop talking about unhappy past experiences. Stop looking for sympathy. Who needs it?

There are two states of consciousness in everyone. They are represented metaphysically by John the Baptist and Jesus Christ. John proclaimed: *"He must increase, but I must decrease."* (John 3:30) John represents the wilderness side of our nature. That is the side of ignorance, old limited concepts in thought. He represents the intellectual concept of Truth which is not yet quickened by the activity of Spirit. Naturally, this consciousness decreases as the light of the higher consciousness, the Jesus Christ consciousness, is shed on the intellect and in the individual.

This change is brought about by turning attention away from the false prophets who proclaim the "Woe is me! Lack! Limitation!" attitudes that may present themselves in guises of short supply, undesirable jobs, and poor relationships, to an awareness that there dwells within a higher Self. The higher consciousness is established by taking daily advantage of all means of spiritual growth presented to you. Some of the great advancers are prayer, meditation, and paying attention to what you say, think, feel, and do!

The ability to discern the real from the illusionary doesn't appear overnight. It is an attitude, a development in consciousness, that must be cultivated and trained, and which emerges in a gradual way. Success and prosperity do not simply happen to you— *they are caused by you!* No one achieves success in any endeavor by building castles in the air. Dreams alone cannot do the work. Neither can a person succeed only if he relies on human strength. True success is assured, however, when you fully rely on the presence and power of God and make positive action to use the power and ideas He has given all.

One whose mind is stayed on God cannot be misled in any manner or by any false presentation imitating Truth. Be aware that your desired good will come into manifestation as fast as your subconscious mind can accept it! If you have been a "negative thinker," or an "I don't have" person, your pictured good may seem so vastly different from what your mind is accustomed to experiencing that it takes some time for the subconscious to absorb the new way of thinking and decide you are definite about being prosperous!

Here is where patience and persistence pay off. Hang in there! If necessary, go the extra mile in holding to your desires and having faith in God. A one-man craft shop cannot produce the same quantities of merchandise as an assembly-line factory. Take one step at a time. Do your thinking clearly. Do your contemplating wisely. Do your deciding definitely. Do your trusting and believing positively and powerfully!

Affirm: *I know the fulfillment of all my needs and desires exists in the cosmic universe. I know that the fulfillment of these needs and desires can come through both known and unknown channels. I know that complete fulfillment is moving toward me now, and I joyfully accept all the good God has for me. I give thanks for abundant prosperity in my life now!*

The "Kingdom of Heaven" Parables

If you delve deeply into a study of the teachings of Jesus, you will find that the content of the whole body of His instructions followed three general categories. Wherever He traveled, Jesus talked about, dealt with, and explained or illustrated through symbolism either the *nature of God, the kingdom of heaven, or healing.* In every instance, the Master encompassed in some manner one or more or all three of these categories of Truth which are available to us.

Upon close observation, it is apparent that all three categories are directed toward helping us where we are *presently.* This is Truth we can use today, regardless of when it was initially presented! Jesus also indicated that He has other things He could tell us besides the nature of God, the kingdom of heaven, and healing, but we wouldn't be able to comprehend or use it yet! *"I have yet many things to say to you, but you cannot bear them now."* (John 16:12)

The nature of God symbolism taught by Jesus is clear. He called God His Father. He referred to *"my Father," "our Father,"* and *"your Father,"* as the relationship of every human being to God. It is a relationship of *oneness.* Jesus also designated the nature of God as Spirit. Then, Jesus called God good, meaning the fullness of the principle of Good. We understand through Truth studies that real prosperity comes from All-Good.

In the healing category, the Truth that healing is a spiritual activity abounds in the Gospels. The various ministrations are available for our perusal, study, and implementation. Any person who is willing can develop a healing consciousness. If one does not have health and wholeness, then that one is not fully prosperous, for prosperity encompasses every aspect of our being and life.

It is in the kingdom of heaven area of Jesus' teachings that He is not literal. Information on this subject is given entirely in parables. It is important to note here that the kingdom of heaven and the kingdom of God are *not* synonymous. The kingdom of God is absolute, omnipresent. It refers to the container of all that is, which is Omnipresence. The kingdom of heaven has to do primarily with man, and it is changeable, variable, and expanding. The kingdom of God is within you. The kingdom of heaven is at hand! And that is relative, not absolute!

Each of the "kingdom" parables brings its own special enlightenment in a particular manner, which can greatly enhance your prosperity awareness. If you wish to do personal reading and reference work with some of these parables, the following chart may be helpful:

Parable	Scripture	Prosperity Analogy
The Sower	Matthew 12:24-30	Cause and Effect
The Mustard Seed	Matthew 13:31, 32	Quantity and Size of Growth

The Leavened Flour   Matthew 13:33   Effectiveness

The Hidden Treasure Matthew 13:44   Divine Principles

The Pearl of Great

Price   Matthew 13:45, 46   Value of Meaning

As you read and study, look for the common denominator running through each parable which denotes, upon reflection, a very real prosperity principle. *Each parable is different, yet similar. Each parable begins with something small and alone and, in some manner, grows either in size, quantity, value, or meaning.* Another important common element is that *the subject of each parable, in its own way, blesses and enriches whoever owns it, touches it, or whomever it touches!* Here are vivid examples that God's good brings prosperity to all!

Now, take the time to look within your nature and determine how you, as a traveler on the path, equate with the information presented in the parables. It is important, if you want to glean the greatest understanding, to parallel these parables with comparable elements in your life. Ask yourself:

What part of me began as something small and alone?

What part of me is growing and expanding?

What part of me is increasing in value day by day?

What treasure was buried, or hidden, within me but now shines forth for all to see and enriches my life and the lives of those I meet?

What part of me have I learned to value above all else?

It seems that the thing Jesus was talking about that fits all these analogies and answers all these questions is your personal, beautiful, individual, growing consciousness of God and Truth. This is the essence of the kingdom of heaven.

Now that you are more aware of the kingdom of heaven, perhaps in a different way, use the awareness to draw increasing awareness. A simple but important experiment is to touch everything you do with the kingdom of heaven aspect of your consciousness— every day's activities, every person with whom you come in contact each day, every situation you experience. Better still, let the kingdom of heaven touch everything you do! If you're working in your home, touch every item in your home with a consciousness of

God. If you are driving to work, touch every passing vehicle, every person, every building, plant, and tree with a God thought. If you are instructing or attending a class, give the class a strong injection of the kingdom of heaven awareness because this energy purifies and blesses and richly and rightly relates to everything it touches. The kingdom of heaven is the one thing that can be yours eternally because it derives from your personal growth within the kingdom of God. And you always have the kingdom of God within you. That's real prosperity! If you lose everything else but still have a kingdom of heaven consciousness, then you shall have all you ever really need or want, because this kind of spiritual consciousness contains all that can become manifest!

An important question is raised here. How can you help the kingdom of heaven within you grow and expand? The answer is: *through personal commitment and effort and use of the knowledge derived from your studies in Truth and, of course, prayer, meditation, love, and thanksgiving.*

The Law of Opportunity

The incarnating soul journeys through matter from the time of its inception as an out-breath of God until it attains perfection. During any earthly lifetime, we contact many teaching experiences, some of them painful because the ego doesn't recognize its own latent powers and potentialities. Encased in the flesh garment, we are beginning to reach toward Christ awareness and stretch further toward Christ consciousness. In ignorance, we fall short of the law of brotherhood and come face to face with the law of cause and effect. Cause and effect operates parallel to another universal law—the law of free will—which I like to acknowledge as the law of opportunity.

Everywhere opportunities abound for the soul who is alert and awake and open to receive. In this present period of Earth history, each of us has opportunities such as have never been seen before. Presented to us daily are more and greater opportunities to grow spiritually than in any previous period in the world's history. Take advantage of what is offered you! Seize each precious opportunity to grow. Do not let a single opportunity pass by unexplored.

What is opportunity? It is a chance to do and to become something splendid! It is heaven's call to you to fulfill your highest destiny!

Oftentimes an occasion that may seem to be fraught with the most difficult elements of the greatest human necessity can prove to be an occasion of tremendous divine opportunity. Turn not away from any experience. At every moment during your life, hidden perhaps from your human view, universal energies are being released into the arena where you meet your daily tasks and work toward mastery. These energies contain the essence of the power supreme and await simply your call to bring even greater assistance to your life experience.

It has been said that struggle adds glory to both men and flowers! When you observe God's creatures performing their functions with courage and endurance, you can be assured as to what mankind, God's human creation, can accomplish with its vastly broader realm of opportunity. Therefore, push forward with courage and zeal, knowing that you are a child of the Most High and that it is God's wish to provide for you the kingdom of heaven and all its transcendent blessings.

Be refreshed daily through loving service. Feel the comfort and sustenance of universal energy flowing through you like a mighty river of continual life, light, love, and power. In the heart of the Eternal, find perfect peace. In tranquillity and serenity of Spirit your inner vision will expand and become open, and you shall see the beauty of life all around you and experience the abundance of a life lived according to Principle.

The highest Truth you presently know is but a half-truth. Think not, my friend, to settle down eternally in any one Truth. Use the understanding of the Truth you now have as you would make use of a tent in which to spend a summer's night. Hasten not, however, to build a house of the present Truth you think you know, lest it become your tomb. When life brings you a faint inkling of the insufficiency of the Truth you presently hold close, and you catch the faintest glimmer of a greater Truth rising on the horizon, weep not. Instead, give thanks to the universe and recognize the cosmic call to pick up thy bed and walk! No matter how far into Truth you feel you have advanced, always remember, there is ever more!

Prosperity Pointers

1. Direct your energies always toward a closer working relationship with God.
2. Recognize that growth begins within you. Don't blame others or outside influences for any personal challenges. See the challenges as opportunities.
3. As in mind, so in manifestation is the law. You cannot reap what you have not sown or grown within yourself. And you have the know-how to separate the wheat from the chaff.
4. Refuse to be limited by facts, experiences, or circumstances. Know the reality!
5. Build a super-fantastic tomorrow by being aware of today's thoughts, feelings, words, and actions!
6. Love yourself! Love your neighbor! Love the universe by seeing the unity of all creation and the abundance everywhere present!
7. Look around you. Find beauty and

joy and invite them to be permanent guests in your house.

8. Listen to your indwelling creative Spirit in quietness many times daily and be guided by the loving whisperings of wisdom from your Christ self.

9. Again, look about you. Give of yourself in all ways and be ready and able to receive graciously. In order to acquire balance, the law of giving and receiving must work in totality.

10. Dwell in the house of the Lord, the kingdom of God, forever!

Rainbow Meditation

Pray always with your heart open to love, for it is through love that the blessings of Spirit are made manifest.

Pray, knowing that love is the way of fulfillment. That which is given in love is received, multiplied, and returned in love.

All that you need of health, abundance, or understanding of the nature of God is within you to be brought forth through your thoughts, words, and deeds of lovingkindness.

Release all fear of ill health, lack, or misunderstanding, and stand upon the solid, holy ground of a loving heart.

Grasp each opportunity to be a living example of the lessons of love as taught by Jesus Christ. Listen to and heed His instruction. Then your heart, mind, and body will be ready to receive the good which is already awaiting your acceptance.

Who Told You So?

*L*et's work with an experiment for a few minutes. Think about some person whom you know. Look at his or her characteristics. Do you consider this person a good human being, or do you see some negative qualities? In an overall analysis, what do you think about this person? Did someone you know imply that this person had undesirable qualities, or did the opinion derive from your own thinking? Who told you so? Whatever you may believe or perceive about a person is only your personal concept of him or her, isn't it! A close friend or relative of the person you are thinking about would behold that individual in a different light perhaps, because his concepts would be in accordance with his own thinking. Should our person in the experiment have "enemies," again, a different concept is formed.

Now, how do you think God sees the person you are thinking about? If all of us are created out of God, would God see evil in His beloved children? I think not. God would be conscious of Himself, expressing as Himself, on many different levels. Pure divine love would be aware of pure divine love, in all and through all. It is true that love is magnified in every heart where it is allowed to enter. Think of the magnitude of the love you could experience right here on Earth, in your daily world and associations, if you forged a conscious chain of love. You would behold no undesirable characteristics in another. Love would tell you the Truth about each person, and your concepts would be totally good. Wouldn't it be a glorious service for humanity to begin a chain of love, allowing it to flow from you, continuing to expand from one person to another until it quickly multiplied and magnified as a resounding force that would be felt throughout the universe?

There seem to be three phases of our being:
1. The inner me, which is God individualized as me.
2. My concept of myself.
3. My concepts expressing outwardly as my body and personal affairs.

My concepts of myself are extremely important, for they manifest my world!

Thought plus feeling equals demonstration! My self-image reproduces itself as *form.* Personal negative concepts produce troubles and limitation. Personal Truth concepts produce all the abundant good that life can encompass.

As we live and work in today's world, we're exposed to myriad experiences of concepts and beliefs. We need to be careful of the things we place our attention upon, because whatever we identify with has the power to influence and change our inner life. So often we react to what is presented rather than taking a split second to "be still, and know that I Am God," to center ourselves in the Truth we know, and then to act accordingly.

How It All Began

In the Garden of Eden allegory we find much metaphysical food for thought. In the Garden were two types of trees: *The tree of life* and *the tree of the knowledge of good and evil.*

And the Lord God commanded the man, saying, "You may freely eat of every tree of the garden; but of the tree of the knowledge of good and evil you shall not eat,

*for in the day that you eat of it you shall
die."* (Genesis 2:16, 17)

The tree of life represents the activity of
Christ or the Holy Spirit from which flow intelligence to the mind, substance to the body,
and life to the entire being. We may partake
of its essence and use it for God's purpose of
good. Apparently the Garden was filled with
such trees, for Adam was told he could eat of
all the trees of the Garden except one. This
Genesis commandment speaks of the vast
abundance of God, in the midst of which
everyone abides.

But in the allegory, Adam and Eve ate also
of the tree of the knowledge of good and evil
and, therefore, had to die. Inasmuch as they
did not have physical form, for they were not
yet *clothed,* the death was to the awareness
of God expressing through them as their constant good. They became conscious of good
and evil where, heretofore, Adam and Eve
had been conscious only of God. Their state
of bliss was lost through their limited thinking about God.

We limit ourselves when we think of any
individual as being good or bad. When we see
good, the full benefit of our blessing often
isn't given, for the "best good" isn't the ulti-

mate. Our true goal is to see the expression of God in each person; we must see the Christ appearing as the individual. Oh, if only we would take the words *I Behold the Christ in You* as our motto for daily living! Through this kind of thinking, we would place no limitations on any person or upon ourselves! This is the whole point of the "Who Told You So?" idea: What you see at any time is only your personal concept!

If you do not inwardly feel at one with God, you may not feel safe and secure, happy and prosperous, healthy and whole. In other words, you may feel naked and exposed to worldly limitations, and that kind of feeling can cause you to be the victim of these untruths. The Adam and Eve aspects of our being must be disciplined and controlled by the Christ aspect in constructive ways.

Mankind isn't yet fully awakened out of the Adam sleep. Even Scripture does not tell us that God awakened Adam. Adam must awaken himself! All limited concepts, all false beliefs, are part of our dream state. Awaken ye that sleep!

Another aspect of the Adam and Eve story is the serpent, or the tempter. This serpent is exemplified by all the human beliefs and concepts coalesced into what is termed "race consciousness." Instead of accepting that what race consciousness whispers is real and true, we give ear to the voice of the Christ within as it questions, "Who told you so?"

Who says you can't be healed? Who says you're too old? Who says you have to be poor? Who says you inherit disease or sickness? Who says the universe isn't unfolding as it should? Who says divine justice no longer prevails? Who says this is good or that is bad? Did God tell you this? Of course not! Rather, God says: *"Come to me, all who labor and are heavy laden, and I will give you rest."* (Matt. 11:28) God says, "It is my good pleasure to give you the kingdom." God says, "Be thou made whole!" God saw His works and called them good!

Remember that God—good—evil are impersonal. They become personal only when they become an active part of the consciousness—a concept—of an individual. You place the name on everything. You call it good or bad! Awakening from the Adam dream state doesn't happen overnight. Individuals are unfolding on many levels of consciousness. Until the whole person—all levels of consciousness—is lifted up to the Christ awareness, old serpents (temptations) will raise their ugly heads and demand attention. When this happens, don't resent it. Don't fight it. See it for what it is, a reappearing temptation trying to entice you to believe something other than what the voice of God tells you. Ask yourself the question, "Who tells me so?" If God doesn't tell you, then pay no attention. Release the thought. Let go and let God.

Breaking Old Habit Patterns

Your future is the result of universal law at work. Your future will be the product of the patterns you follow today. As you study the laws of human nature and the laws of God and observe how they operate, you can, with a great degree of accuracy, predict your future. As you travel the journey of life, the laws of human nature usually prevail and determine what is going to happen next in human affairs. But God's law of grace can transcend the laws of human nature.

Let's claim some of the attitudes of Jesus as our own. Jesus could foresee that people usually acted according to human nature. He knew that the products of a pattern didn't change. Through His teachings He sought to help mankind realize that when the pattern was changed, and it could be, then the end result would be different. He went about in His ministry planting positive seed ideas that would sprout strong thoughts to promote personal growth of all who would hear. Let's look at some seed ideas:

1. *The present, for me, embodies all my past. My future depends upon the clear perception of the immediate vision.*

2. *The will to Christ consciousness is galvanized by divine love.*

3. *Each life experience can lead me onward as a stepping-stone, or I can allow it to present a stumbling block. The concept is mine.*

4. *Humility, strength, awareness, and sincerity of purpose are my gifts to humanity today.*

5. *The radiance of my heart leads me to understanding and peace.*

6. *My soul has purpose, power, and will. These three are needed on the way to liberation.*

7. *I press forward toward the goal of fuller service.*

8. *I know that I am the soul whose nature is light and love and selflessness.*
9. *I manifest my divine plan and am at one with every aspect of life.*
10. *I stand erect through love and light divine!*

The Power of the Gentle Touch

From a tender age, most of us have been guided to work hard if we wish to be successful. We hear phrases such as "putting the shoulder to the wheel," "laying the ax to the grindstone," and "putting the hand to the plow." These entreaties are encouragements for us to do what needs to be done. The admonition to work hard is good, but it is only a half-truth. *Hard work alone never brought success to anyone!* My grandfather used to say, "The person who *perspires* the most isn't necessarily the one who *acquires* the most!" Another vital factor is needed—faith! Scripture tells us in James 2:26 that *faith apart from works is dead.* And work without faith is futile.

The person who works diligently, faithfully, and happily toward a definite goal achieves real success. The person who also understands that his real work in life is that of personal growth, and remembers that his vocation is merely an avenue through which he may accomplish the real work, loves what he does and cooperates with God and is successful. Thomas Edison is credited with saying, "I never worked a day in my life. It was all play, because I put my imagination into it!" Thus, it seems *what we do* isn't the primal factor, rather, *how we do it!*

When I worked in the furniture industry, my supervisor placed great emphasis on quality control throughout the manufacturing plant. He would walk through the factory, pausing in the various departments, minutely inspecting the construction processes of the furniture on the line, and advise the workers good-naturedly to "take it easy" and give the items being made the "gentle touch." His favorite comment to sales personnel was, "The surest way to be happy and successful is to apply the 'gentle touch' in everything you do."

Golf partners have often reminded me to "take it easy," and I noticed that the drive that went farthest down the fairway occurred when I swung the club with the greatest ease.

The phrase, "take it easy," is a long-standing byword of practically every successful athletic coach. The great concert pianist plays with flowing ease. The champion swimmer glides through the water with seemingly little effort. The brilliant actor speaks the words and blends the action in a harmony of sound and movement. The person whose life flows like a happy melody is the one who doesn't worry or fret about getting things done. He simply does them! He doesn't rush about frantically, often creating additional problems through his hurry. He knows that God is in charge of his life, so he goes about doing what needs to be done by him, calmly and quietly, and applies the gentle touch. He believes the promise of Scripture in James 3:17 that says: *"But the wisdom from above is first pure, then peaceable, gentle, open to reason, full of mercy and good fruits, without uncertainty or insincerity."*

As a child, I remember reading an old fable that described a contest held between the sun and the wind to determine which was the stronger. One day, the wind was blustering and roaring and bragging about how great and strong he was. The sun, going about doing his thing and perhaps getting a little tired of all the noise, challenged the wind to a contest. The sun said to the wind, "I know how we can decide, once and for all, which of us is the stronger."

The wind huffed and blew some more and asked, "How?"

The sun smiled and indicated a traveler who was walking along the road below with his cloak pulled tightly around him as a buffer against the wind and cold. "Brother Wind, whichever one of us can compel the traveler to remove his cloak shall be regarded as the stronger."

The wind agreed and declared he would be first to try. So, the wind blew, and he blew, and he blew some more. The traveler wrapped his cloak even more closely about him and turned up his collar. Finally, the wind gave up, admitting his failure, but proclaiming that the sun would also fail.

The sun smiled and began to beam his warming rays gently on the traveler on the road below. He didn't struggle to accomplish his purpose, he simply allowed himself to be what he was! He let his beautiful light shine! Soon, the traveler began to become warm. He loosened the cloak, turned his collar down and continued walking. After a few minutes, the traveler became so warm that little drops of perspiration appeared on his forehead and he removed his cloak and tossed it across his arm!

This story reminds me of how effortlessly Jesus went about His ministry. We don't read of Him dashing across the countryside in a hurry, or being filled with anxiety. He never seemed to waste thought, feeling, or emotional energy. A cameo look at the Master is found in II Corinthians, chapter 10, verse 1, when Paul said: *I, Paul, myself entreat you, by the meekness and gentleness of Christ...*"

Jesus taught how the individual may attain mastery, the dominion that is one's personal divine birthright. In the third Beatitude, Jesus said: *"Blessed are the meek, for they shall inherit the earth!"* (Matt. 5:5) Meekness, as given in this Scripture, means to cultivate a mental attitude of willingness. We become willing to let God guide and direct us or, as we often proclaim in Unity, we let go and let God!

When wrongly interpreted, meekness can cause one to become a victim of power-hungry people, governments, or organizations. When rightly interpreted, meekness frees us from the bondage of dependency on any person, place, thing, government, or organization. The meekness and gentleness of the Master, His constant, calm serenity, were evidence of His tremendous faith in the allness and goodness of God.

A lot of people in these days allow themselves to live under pressure brought on by worry and anxiety. There is no pressure in God's divine plan. There is nothing for us to fear or be anxious about. God is still in command of the universe. Wherefore, then, is the reason for worry and concern over the outcome of this situation or that condition? A teacher said once, "Do your best and leave the rest to God." That is excellent advice.

The gentle touch isn't a sign of weakness. It is closely akin to humility and meekness. *There is power in the gentle touch, for it is the Godly touch.* It is the way to attain beauty and perfection. Look about you. Observe the gentle touch throughout nature. See how silently nature moved over the land to bring the green of the grass and new buds. Do you remember staring across a valley of green apple orchards that turned white with blossoms almost overnight in springtime? Can you recall a quiet winter morning when you looked out your window in surprise at a blanket of fine and glistening snow covering the ground? Your grade school science class taught that the Earth swings in its orbit as gently as a feather in a soft breeze. These are but some of the mighty works God achieves through the gentle touch!

Spirit can and will move mightily on your behalf when you place all that you are at its disposal. The promise: "... *in quietness and in trust shall be your strength*" is a reminder that God is the only power in the universe active in your life. This power of God expresses itself most effectively as love. Apply the gentle touch. Follow the route to success. In the beginning, when God said, "Let there be ... " He spoke the Word. He didn't struggle and strive to bring about His creation. There was nothing to struggle or strive against. God was the allness in and through everything. This is true today. Learn to minimize your personal desires and let God fulfill His desire in you. This is the way to success and happiness through the gentle touch.

Achieving Inner Security On Your Own!

How many people do you know who really feel secure? The feeling of security or of insecurity stems primarily from a person's basic approach to life. If you are unfamiliar with your own innate greatness and the infinite divinity within you just waiting to be released, then you may tend to magnify problem situations and difficulties rather than looking beyond appearances to the reality. One of the primary reasons for any feeling of insecurity is that one looks at the externals of life as *causes,* instead of realizing that they are merely effects.

Know that there is no separation between you and the omnipresent power of God. You are immersed in an infinite ocean of life. It constantly permeates the world in which you live, move, and have your being. The moment you recognize its existence, its reality, the power and wisdom of this infinite potential become potent and active in your life.

The wise and fastidious musician places his Stradivarius in a velvet-lined case and stores it in a moderately heated room. If this were not done, at the time of his concert the musician would have a poorly tuned instrument, and regardless of his great genius, he would be at a disadvantage in having no medium through which to pour his artistry to the responsive ears of his audience.

So it is with your consciousness of God. You may listen to what people say, but the *experiencing* of the consciousness of God is an inside job. When this activity takes place, you will experience immediately a marvelous feeling of inner security, and discover the serenity and calm peace that flood your soul and keep you ever the master over all situations.

To believe is to accept something as true! However, many people believe things which are absolutely false and, consequently, they suffer to the extent of their belief! If, for example, you believe that Seattle is a city in New Mexico, and address a letter to a friend accordingly, the letter will go astray or it will be returned to you by the post office.

Two worlds run parallel to one another. One is the world of cause; the other is the world of effect. You, as a creator, have access to the world of cause through the use of thought and feeling, and constantly generate in your world the myriad patterns that project their images, like monstrous shadows, into the world of effect where man, in the outer consciousness, dwells. But if man were denied the opportunity of experimenting and learning through the use of energy in this realm of cause, he would be but a puppet and not a potential god!

Right where you are is the place you can do the greatest work now. The place where you are is the place God wants you to be. Do your work here with joy and appreciation. Whenever you feel the urge to do "big things" for God or man, begin doing the little things in your life better. Your work is God's work, and regardless of how trivial the day's activities may appear, all is important to the divine plan. Give thanks for all the Truth you have learned. Praise your ability to work with yourself and grow spiritually. That which is done in a spirit of joy is always done well, and everything that is done well invariably leads to greater works.

You reach the point where you tap the still, small voice within and go forward under your own momentum, through the dictates of your own expanding consciousness. The journey to inner serenity and security is accomplished step by step. One thought at a time. One feeling at a time. One action at a time. Life is made up of little things. Everything that exists in the universe is composed of minute cells which are too small to be seen by the naked eye. God makes great things by adding together a host of little things. So can you! This is the principle of divine construction!

Luther Burbank fell in love with plants. Edison fell in love with invention. Ford fell in love with motor cars. Kettering fell in love with research. The Wright brothers fell in love with airplanes. God fell in love with you! Someone has truly said, "Be careful what you set your heart on, for it will surely come true." Those who harness their hearts to mighty tasks often see their dreams become realities.

See yourself free of any limiting or dis-ease-producing obstacle. Refuse to acknowledge any difficulty or situation as having power over you. Truly it has none! If inharmony is created in any manner in your life, it is because you have said yes to the situation. *You told you so!* Stop right now. Refuse to give consent ever again to any undesirable thought, feeling, action, or situation in your life. You don't want temporary relief. You want to put an end to all undesirable conditions once and for all time. Why take an aspirin for temporary relief from a headache when you have the opportunity to eliminate the cause of the headache? It can be done. Put forth the effort and be amazed at the transformation that takes place within you and in your world.

Rainbow Meditation

Be still, my child, and know that I AM God;
That I, who from my bosom gave you life,
Will ever guard and protect you from earthly
strife.
So that you may know that we are one,
Within your heart a gentle threefold flame
Of love, wisdom, and power burns brightly.
And in your precious calls to me,
Your great sincerity will draw forth the power
To raise all life into my Light.
Be still, my child, and know that I AM God,
And whenever life's burdens seem hard to
bear,
It is then that I shall pour forth into your
world
My sustaining and gentle love,
To hold you steadfast
To the appointed way.
I bring you the power of gentle comfort,
To bless all of life,
That peace on Earth shall come to stay.

Be still, sweet soul, and know that I AM God,
And mold you to my own great design,
That you may fulfill your divine plan.
Deep within your heart, the Christ knows.
So, raise your eyes to beyond the skies.
Call forth my love.
Use its power to do my will,
To bless all of mankind
With the light of Truth that shines forever.

Rainbow Promises for Your Total Unfoldment

I will instruct you and teach you the way you should go; I will counsel you with my eye upon you. (Psalms 32:8)

"... no one will take your joy from you." (John 16:22)

"... according to the promise that I made you.... My Spirit abides among you; fear not." (Hag. 2:5)

You shall be a crown of beauty in the hand of the Lord, and a royal diadem in the hand of your God. (Isa. 62:3)

Honor the Lord with your substance and with the first fruits of all your produce; then your barns will be filled with plenty, and your vats will be bursting with wine. (Prov. 3:9, 10)

For by me your days will be multiplied, and years will be added to your life. (Prov. 9:11)

"For I the Lord do not change...." (Mal. 3:6)

"... fear not, for I am with you and will bless you...." (Gen. 26:24)

"Come to me, all who labor and are heavy laden, and I will give you rest." (Matt. 11:28)

And God is able to provide you with every blessing in abundance, so that you may always have enough of everything and may provide in abundance for every good work. (II Cor. 9:8)

"... give, and it will be given to you; good measure, pressed down, shaken together, running over, will be put into your lap. For the measure you give will be the measure you get back." (Luke 6:38)

Out of the Lonely Crowd

*I*f you took the time to sit down today and make a list of all the good things you wanted from life, your list would most likely include peace of mind, accomplishment, financial success, and prosperity in all areas of your life, as well as inner security, a good job, compatible companionship, and expressions of love. Possession of these joys of living would, you think, bring you out of the lonely crowd of those seeking happiness.

There is a way all these things can and will manifest for you. It is described by the wise person who once stated that in order to be a radiant, effective, and prosperous child of God, it is necessary to love and appreciate, first yourself, then others, and to forgive yourself and others. Yes, forgiveness is essential! Forgiveness brings into manifestation the healing consciousness which transmutes all errors into pure divine energy. The old is made new, born again.

I'm certain all of us can think of friendships that have been severed because of lack of forgiveness. We have seen marriages fail because of an unforgiving attitude, and we have seen businesses ruined because someone refused to release ill feelings and hurts.

Forgiveness means to cleanse, to blot out, or to restore. Truly, in its deepest expression, forgiveness means a restoration of all conditions and associations to the purity of beingness that existed before transgressions were perceived. As long as anyone is unable to forgive, that one has allowed a tremendous blockage to manifest in the divine flow of love into his life! Any blockage is caused by the "little me" aspect of self.

When asked, "Why is the action of forgiveness so vital?" the answer comes forth loud and clear: Forgiveness is a process of giving up the false for the true, erasing concepts from your mind and body. It is through forgiveness that true healing on all levels is accomplished. Forgiveness removes the errors of the mind, and harmony results.

The first step to take in forgiveness is repentance. It is a change of mind. It is turning away from all things as they appear to be and

179

turning within to the Truth of God. Forgiveness is more than being "sorry." It is the acquiring of a new attitude which results in a sincere desire to do better. It is the ability to see the perfection of God in process of being brought forth in all individuals, according to each person's spiritual understanding.

We have all made mistakes. We have made decisions and taken action which were not fully for the highest and best in life expression. Perhaps we have mentally kicked ourselves for such decisions. You have punished yourself enough! Your soul has paid the price. Whatever the obstacle, drop it! Forget it! Release it! Let love's healing energy do its perfect work of regeneration.

Spiritually, we are still as children. But we are children of God! The Christ Spirit lives within each of us, leading us in the way we should advance for perfect development. Perhaps someone did stumble and fall across your path in your sphere of influence. Perhaps he offended your little human dignity. Is it not better to see that person for what he is—a son of the Most High who has merely wandered off course! Be big enough to forgive. You cannot be offended unless you accept the offense. To accept any idea of offense means you have crossed the boundary of the radiation of God's idea of oneness with all creation. When you cross the boundary of Christ thinking into human thinking, you fail to see clearly or correctly. Get back in tune with yourself.

Pause now. Ask yourself whether you are experiencing poor relationships, disorder, inharmony, or lack. If so, then hold closely within your consciousness the affirmation: *Divine love, acting through me, blesses and forgives.* Divine love is a mighty power waiting to be used. It abides within you and within every human being. It easily responds to itself in you and in others. It has been described as the most powerful thing in the world, and yet, it is the easiest to use! It responds quickly to your thoughts, feelings, and words. You alone hold the key to release the activity of divine love in your world. Speak the word that sets it into motion, and come out of the lonely crowd and be the radiant, shining light of God you truly are!

Establish a Positive Mental Attitude in Your Life

Napoleon Hill and W. Clement Stone are two well-known businessmen who have built the idea of a positive mental attitude into a mighty success method which is helping thousands of people. The crux of their method is simple Truth: What your mind can conceive, your mind can achieve! And it all begins with a positive mental attitude.

Each day of the year has 1,440 minutes. Invest *one percent* of that time in a study, thinking, and planning session with a better life as your targeted goal and you will be astounded at how those fourteen minutes daily help you become better acquainted with the God side of yourself! As surely as day follows night, you will begin to feel the mighty dynamics at your command.

A positive mental attitude releases everything in your mind that could be detrimental to your highest good. Allow yourself to see the complete and wonderful picture of holistic good. Dwell upon that which is enduring, which was before time, and which shall remain when time is no more. Turn from the conscious thoughts that analyze, accept, and reject, and measure and equate to the center of life and light Jesus implied when He said: *"I am the light of the world . . . . "* (John 8:12) Turn from the demanding powers and thoughts of the intellect to the quiet, serene, purposeful realization of God's presence and power within you.

One God thought can transmute a thousand negations. One sincere prayer may become the channel of a healing. Where there is weakness shall abide perfect strength. Where there has been discord shall emerge perfect harmony when one dwells in the presence of God. As a special attunement with the healing energies of love, take a moment and become one with these prayer thoughts:

Father-Mother God, illuminator of all,
May the mists from my eyes be cleared,
And may my vision expand to behold the
    Christ
In every soul I meet.

Father-Mother God, omnipotent pres-
    ence in all,
May all shackles of the small confines of
    self
Fall away, and expose the selfless life in
    You,

Allowing Truth to permeate all mankind.

Father-Mother God, fountainhead of
love,
May my life stream be eternally
dedicated
To living a life of gentle, enfolding,
presence
Through the greatness You behold in all.

Father-Mother God, constant source of
all good,
May I ever grasp the hand of my fellow-
man
In deepest sincerity, seeking no claim of
reward
Save that of eternal love and life flowing
from You.

Father-Mother God, resurrecting Spirit
in all,
May I acknowledge with the Christ who
in Jesus dwelled:
". . . and I, when I am lifted up from the
earth,
will draw all men to myself." Amen.

The Vital Life-Force

You do not stand alone as an isolated and independent creation, but blend with all manifested life. You float in and draw every breath of your existence from universal substance which, to your physical eyes, is invisible, but which, in reality, is the only light, life, and intelligence. You have within you a coursing stream of currents of dynamic energies of many types, all of them accounting for your vital processes, your urges, impulses, motives, moods, thoughts, emotions, dreams, and ideal visions.

This life-force, which gives you the power of awareness and doingness, is the same which regulates every living thing. This life-force is intelligent and not a blind and brutish activity. It regulates you and every other living thing to breathe certain quantities of various elements in order to sustain life, to convert food substances into energy needed for bodily growth and repair, to manufacture blood, secretions, extractions, and to distribute these compounds throughout your human organism for nourishment, new cells, and vital energy for physical activities.

It knows in constant and exact proportion

what, when, and how to do a thousand things necessary to a human organism, perfectly and simultaneously. Your life is in the keeping of this tremendous intelligence every second. You trust this great intelligence to keep your heart beating. You close your eyes at night and sleep in the confidence and trust that all systems will continue to "go" during the night. And life goes on! The vital life-force takes care of you and loves you. In the making of the molecules of your body, it had to create atoms, those sparks of cosmic fire which mankind has come to realize contain within themselves the same energy as the sun and all the galaxies. All of this activity is a vast process of love.

You, dear friend, are the mighty repository of everything that has gone before from the dawn of creation and when what we call time and space were birthed from the radiance of the Absolute. Yes, you possess within the boundaries of your body, mind, and soul every type, kind, quantity, and intensity of intelligent, radiant energy that may be necessary to provide you with exactly what you need at this time.

How, then, could you be lonely, afraid, or disconsolate? This remarkable divine plan is a perfect part of the larger pattern for the tremendous good of everyone. It isn't something that is separate or apart for you alone. It has ramifications and interweavings that flow in and through all persons you meet and all the events of life that come your way. Thus it would seem that the best way to place yourself in harmony with this great universal outworking is to accept with radiant acquiescence every individual and event drawn into your world, seeing them as the perfect instruments for the perfect unfoldment of all good. Harmony within brings harmony without.

Send forth a prayer for drawing to you all those who may be helped by you, and for all those for whom your help is needed in order to express your life together with them.

Yes, There Is a Plan!

If someone asked you today, "What is your plan of action for the balance of this life expression?" what would you answer? At this point in your personal growth and unfoldment, are you aware of your divine plan for this embodiment and how you can implement its unfoldment? Are you underestimating the unlimited potentialities within yourself, or are you beginning to more knowingly put them to work?

Shakespeare wrote: *"There is a destiny that shapes our end, rough hew it how we will."* And my grandmother said, "God gave us two ends—one to think with, and one to sit on. The degree of unfoldment of one's divine plan depends on which end is used most!" Scripture tells us in Romans 8:28-30:

We know that in everything God works for good with those who love him, who are called according to his purpose. For those whom he foreknew he also predestined to be conformed to the image of his Son, in order that he might be the first-born among many brethren. And those whom he predestined he also called; and those whom he called he also justified; and those whom he justified he also glorified.

Very definitely, a form of predestination is depicted here. Could this be mention of the divine plan for every individual? Let's look further in Scripture to Ephesians 1:3-5:

Blessed be the God and the Father of our Lord Jesus Christ, who has blessed us in Christ with every spiritual blessing in the heavenly places, even as he chose

us in him before the foundation of the world, that we should be holy and blameless before him. He destined us in love to be his sons through Jesus Christ, according to the purpose of his will . . . .
Also, Ephesians 1:9, 10:

For he has made known to us in all wisdom and insight the mystery of his will, according to his purpose which he set forth in Christ as a plan for the fulness of time, to unite all things in him, things in heaven and things on earth.

These Scriptures mean, to me, that there is an *ultimate goal* or *divine plan* established for every person who is born into this world. Individuals may not realize this Truth and knowingly work with it, but just the same, everyone has a divine destiny! How we move forward to meet that destiny depends upon individual freewill choices.

Prior to moving forward into physical, incarnate expression, we were created by God with the purpose of ultimately "putting on the garment of the Christ." The day of awakening is at hand. He who baptizes with fire (the Holy Spirit) is among us. The identical fire which found voice and spoke to Moses in the burning bush is awaiting with loving anticipation the awakening in every human soul. It is the fire that lighted the darkness for the children of Israel after the initiate kings no longer ruled Egypt and the usurpers had taken authority into their own selfish hands. It is the fire that descended in the form of a dove from heaven to bring peace to men who had refused to accept it. It is the "tongue of fire" which sat upon the Apostles on the day of Pentecost.

Although we may suppress the gentle urgings of our divine plan by getting overly involved in daily experiences, we cannot extinguish the flame of innate divinity that burns continually. One step at a time is the divinity growth formula. Life isn't made up totally of big things. It is also made up of seconds, pennies, ounces, grains of sand, blades of grass, and atoms. Man is made up of all the thoughts he dwells upon all day long. Can you not see this to be correct in your daily life?

I'm reminded of the story of an old stone mason who was once laying a rock wall in the garden of a large estate. The wall had a natural expression and was a thing of great beauty in its unfoldment. The owner of the estate, walking about his grounds, noticed the old stone mason and became intrigued by the intense care with which the old man worked. The mason spent as much time selecting and placing the smaller stones as he did the larger ones.

The estate owner finally asked him, "Friend, wouldn't the work on the wall proceed much faster if you used only the larger stones?"

"Most certainly, sir," the wise old fellow replied. "But, you see, I'm building for beauty and quality and endurance, not for speed!" After a few minutes, the mason added, "Sir, these stones are like men. Many small ones are needed to support the big ones and hold them in place. If you leave out the smaller stones, then the big ones will have no support and they will fall down."

So it is with life and the unfolding of our individual divine plans. It is the cohesion of many small and beautiful thoughts and feelings and actions, one upon one, cemented together by love, that creates the well-balanced life. It is the total of the little things in life that create the wholeness of an embodiment, just as pennies add up to dollars.

We are told in Scripture that in everything God works for good. There is no one, absolutely no one, and no thing present in our lives today—whether in the family circle, the business world, social activities, or wher-ever—that is not here for a definite purpose which is to give us opportunities for growth and spiritual development. According to the universal law of love and attraction, we draw to ourselves the types of persons with the characteristics or the personalities we need at the time.

Another passage in Scripture says: *If God is for us, who is against us?* (Romans 8:31) Also in Romans 8, verse 35: *Who shall separate us from the love of Christ?* God's promises and love are like the cement used by the old stone mason to build his beautiful wall. Each follows his divine plan by blending together all the "bigs" and "littles" of life's experiences. Sometimes when the "powers and principalities" may seem to execute un-due pressures, we are then called upon by life to put into practice all the Truth we know and believe.

On occasion I've been asked, "But isn't it certain that some folks are destined to be great, to do splendid works, and that the hand of God beckons them to be torchbearers for the world? My reply is, "I doubt it." Let's look for a moment, as an example, at the life of Thomas Edison. If we were to think that Edison was destined to be a great wizard of electricity, this would seem to imply that he functioned under a special dispensation and had available for his use certain gifts or aids which were not offered or possessed by the average individual. So what happens?

Expand your understanding. Observe Edison. Look at all the failures he experienced in completing his experiments. Numerous times he attempted to accomplish something, only to come against an obstacle. Yes, it is true that during his lifetime he dedicated and developed himself toward things scientific. *That was his freewill choice.* From the beginning, he functioned under a personal desire that shaped his destiny in this Earth life. His interest, his personal will, his faith in his work, all his faculties played a great part in developing his ability. Finally, through perseverance, he succeeded!

You have the same attributes of interest, will, and faith, and all of your twelve faculties are at your disposal. We are all created equally in divine love; but as we grow, we develop certain personal attributes that others may not exhibit in this particular life journey. But all have the same potentials deep within.

Yes, there is a plan! There is a divine design within each person which continually inspires one forward, which whispers in the soul, "Yes, there's more!" We are especially predestined to put on the consciousness of the Christ at some point in our spiritual evolution, and to become spiritually awakened as our elder brother Jesus said we could.

When one begins to realize that beyond our daily lives there is an eternal plan and purpose, then life takes on a new, exciting meaning. Cressy Morrison, former president of the New York Academy of Science, believes that mathematical law can prove that our universe was designed and executed by divine intelligence.

Dr. Morrison discusses, for instance, the eel, and points out that even that lowly creature is a marvelous demonstration of intricate planning and purpose.

Eels from all over the world at maturity go to the Gulf Stream off Bermuda to breed. From all the rivers and oceans of the world they come to that particular place. From the Volga in Russia and from the Mississippi; from the Amazon in South America and from the Chattahoochee; from Lake Michigan and from the Sea of Japan, they all come, Dr. Morrison says.

Then, after having given birth to their young, they die. But the newborn eels return to the same river, lake, pond, or ocean from where their mothers came. No eel has ever made a mistake as far as the fishermen around the world have discovered! Dr. Morrison says you cannot explain this activity without a divine intelligence, which we call God. And if God would so carefully plan and guide so clearly the lowly eel, how much more has He done and will He do for His highest creation—you and me!

Rainbow Meditation

In a moment of deep inner silence, I heard a gentle voice whisper, "Beloved, dare to make the break out of the lonely crowd. There is a wonderful plan for your life. A magnificent purpose resounds through your unfoldment. Release and let go of your old outdated and outworn self! Dare to be reborn in the brilliance of the free Spirit, filled and motivated with universal energy flowing direct from the heart of God!"

Fascinated, I listened. "Beloved, dare to loose old patterns of expression, old habits of weakness and death, old memories of destruction. Dare to witness the activity of divine love expressing through you as perfect life as it restores, rejuvenates, and regenerates every cell of your being! Live in the wholeness of Spirit, and direct your light essence for the healing and uplifting of the world!"

Wow! I wondered. Do I dare? The voice continued, "Beloved, go beyond your present understanding. Exceed your now conscious-ness of Truth. Be fully immersed in your divine blueprint through all good "on earth as it is in heaven." *You carry within the keys to the kingdom. Use them to open all doors of Christ expression and to direct the wonder and effectiveness of the spiritual gifts you possess into your working knowledge.*"

In expectation, I remained silent, listening. "Beloved, dedicate yourself to love. Watch as love dissolves undesirable situations, un-wanted circumstances, and all thoughts and feelings of a negative nature. Dare to be magnificent! Dare to be a self-renewing temple of the living God! Dare to be beauty, harmony, light, and music as I created you to be! Remember, I have loved you with an ever-lasting love!*"

Joy filled my heart as I asked, "Who are You? Who is saying this to me?"

And from infinity within came the answer, "I AM!"

Overcoming Obstacles

*O*nce upon a time, on a glorious day, a mythical king reviewed his vast kingdom and felt quite benevolent. His wise men had recently extolled the virtues of being a good giver and receiver as an absolute opportunity to lay up treasure in the heaven-world of the gods. Having decided to put the principle into practice, the king called one of his bravest soldiers to come before him and be rewarded for outstanding duty performed. As the old soldier knelt before the throne, a servant placed before him a magnificently engraved golden bowl. One glance assured the soldier the bowl was the creation of a master craftsman and worth a fortune.

The king, gesturing for the soldier to accept the bowl, said, "Brave man, receive this gift as a symbol of my appreciation for your courage and great dependability on the fields of battle."

Overwhelmed with the immensity of what

was happening in his life, the soldier slowly dropped his head and whispered, "Oh, no, your Majesty! I cannot accept such a treasure. Truly, it is too great a gift for me to receive!"

The king stroked his beard in contemplation for a moment, looked at the bowed head before him, and gently replied, "Perhaps, my good man. But please remember that it is not too great a gift for me to give!"

The soldier, looking at the gift from his personal consciousness, felt that the value of the golden bowl far exceeded his idea of self-worth. The king's wisdom, however, taught the soldier to look at life's complete picture. This little story contains several Truth lessons. For now, let's look at an analogy.

Your radiant inner light is like the golden bowl, magnificently created by a master craftsman and shining in all its beauty. You are the soldier. God is the wise king. A tremendous free gift is offered to you. Are you willing to accept it? You may admire the gift from a distance, viewing it from all angles. You may even touch and hold the gift. Surely, you'll tell your best friend about it! But will you acknowledge it as yours? Or will you stare blankly and ask, "Who me?"

Take an action step now to burst through this limiting mental block. In I Timothy, chapter 4, verse 14, Paul admonishes Timothy: *Do not neglect the gift you have . . . .*

Acceptance of the gift of the Christ presence within you changes your behavior in a profound way. When you repent, or change your mind, from believing that outer conditions have power to knowing that a power greater than anything you've ever known previously is within:

You no longer run scared.

You become compassionate and sincere, and many are drawn to your light.

You become serene and at peace with yourself and the world.

You turn increasingly toward a closer working relationship with God.

You recognize that true growth begins within you, and you stop blaming others or outside influences for any personal challenge.

You love yourself, your neighbor, and your universe by seeing the unity of all creation.

You look about and find joy, beauty, abundance, and wonderful life everywhere at all times.

You refuse to be limited by outer facts, ex-

periences, or circumstances.

You build a super-fantastic tomorrow by being aware of today's thoughts, words, feelings, and actions!

You listen to your indwelling creative Spirit in quietness many times daily and allow yourself to be guided by the loving wisdom whisperings.

You give of yourself in all ways and are constantly ready and able to receive graciously.

You never again squeeze the cactus!

Now, whatever do I mean by that last statement?

Returning to Unity Village is always a marvelous experience. On one such trip, I shared, with a minister friend, my inner feelings that I knew God was absolute Good. Yet, at the moment, I was experiencing difficulty when I looked about me and saw people in pain. I seemed to be facing a paradox that wouldn't quite focus. It was like looking through a camera with the lens slightly out of adjustment. She shared with me a story that brought the focus into sharp clarity.

A member who had been attending her church for several years experienced a tragedy. A much loved nineteen-year-old daughter was killed in a traffic accident. The pain, grief, and self-pity that the mother felt completely overshadowed the Truth she knew. The mother sought the strength to deal with the crisis and came to talk one day. As the woman expressed her pain through tears, she was comforted by the presence of the minister. After the minister listened for a while, she commented, "All right, this event has happened. Let's seek to gain some understanding from it. And for a moment, I wish to sidetrack to something else."

The minister then gestured toward a small potted cactus on her desk. She took the cactus and placed it in the mother's hand. The mother was surprised, puzzled, and a little shocked at what was happening.

The minister asked, "Does it hurt to hold the cactus?"

"Well, no," the mother answered. "I'm aware that it's in my hand. You can hold a cactus without pain."

"You're right," the minister smiled. "Now, I want you to squeeze the cactus with your free hand!"

Of course the woman wouldn't perform this action, for she knew what would happen. If she squeezed the cactus, her whole hand would be in agony! The point made to the mother, and to myself, was that sometimes life situations bring us emotional cacti to hold. We're moving along in our daily routine. Some event transpires, and lo and behold, there's a prickly cactus in our life. *And what we generally do with an emotional cactus is squeeze and squeeze and squeeze!* The pain then becomes so great that we can't understand how God, who is absolute Good, can allow this to happen to us!

What we fail to realize is that life brought us the cactus, but we're the ones doing the squeezing, not God. If we will be fully honest and recognize Truth, as we look more closely at this idea of emotional pain or this cactus that has been placed in our feeling nature, the first thing we can recognize is that *God didn't put it there.*

I totally believe that God is absolute Good and that the will of God for me and for my life is also absolute good.

I also believe that suffering is an experience in my house of living that is brought about by some form of human friction. I can look at a hurting situation, recognize it's there, and take the proper steps toward solution. Sometimes, when trying to understand a spiritual Truth, it is good to observe the physical world, for everything in the physical is a reflection of adherence to, or misalignment with, spiritual principles.

We are growing in awareness of the oneness with our Father-Mother Creator. If the activity of loving parents caring for their children in the physical world is observed, we get an idea of God caring for us in the spiritual world. A loving parent would never force a child to experience pain. Rather, we teach our children things to do to avoid having to experience pain. A loving parent seeks to protect the child from things that caused pain for the parent. The parent seeks to guide the child, watch over his actions, so the child doesn't make the same mistakes as the parent. Children often make their own unique mistakes, but the pitfalls are known by the parent and guidance is given. We desire happiness for our children. A home and good food are provided for them. Children are taught the laws of the physical world. They are told about crossing streets and honoring other rules of safety. The same is done for us by our God-Parents in a spiritual way, on a spiritual level. As we give our children freedom to grow, so does God give us freedom to grow.

Jesus tells us: *"Take my yoke upon you, and learn from me; for I am gentle and lowly in heart, and you will find rest for your souls. For my yoke is easy, and my burden is light."* (Matthew 11:29, 30) One of the key thoughts in that Scripture is the statement, *"I am gentle."* Isn't the I AM of each of us gentle? It never forces us. It doesn't intrude. Yet, when we take the time to become still and direct attention to that spark of God within, our Christ self, it offers every assistance. The minute we turn to it in gentle strength, it helps us find the answer to the question, the fulfillment of the need.

Then, if we are holding an emotional cactus, the I AM lets us hold the cactus gently and observe, rather than squeeze and feel the pain. Also, as we hold the cactus and continue to commune with the I AM, we will find a way not only to hold it, but to use our other hand to put it aside. *We can release the cactus completely!* In so doing, we have truly let go and let God take charge. Sometimes I laugh at Rebecca because my human is very sure it knows the right way to do most things. I may find myself saying, "Okay, I'll let go and let God . . . but I'll do the driving!" This is the time to remember that the passenger side is extremely comfortable when God is allowed to drive! In this manner, our course is straight and clear.

In every parable, in every healing, in every action that Jesus took when working with others, the person was required to do something, even if it was to simply stretch forth a hand, or to take up his bed and walk, or to ask and you then receive.

The Lure of the Depths

Occasionally, someone will say, "Well, I simply can't continue. The situation is hopeless. I've reached the point of no return." This is great, because if a person makes this statement—and means it—often that person is ready to be helped! On occasions of this nature, I've observed a person surrender what he believes to be the problem and, in its stead, accept the awareness of the presence of God and follow through by allowing God to express through him as a fulfillment of the need. This point of no return seems to be the bottom line, the end of the road, the pits! If someone hasn't reached this place in consciousness yet, he will stumble back into the experience until he gets truly tired of the depths and decides to do something about it!

Reaching a place in an experience that seems to be the point of no return is actually a positive step forward into growth. This can be the time when one does let go and let God. The choice is always with the individual.

A few years ago an attorney in Florida, whose favorite sport was deep-sea diving, decided to try to break the free-diving record of five years' standing. He entered the water off the coast of Miami and, with the aid of an artificial lung strapped to his back, began his descent. At a depth of 306 feet below the surface, he topped the record for anyone who had made the dive and returned alive. He continued to dive. At a depth of 400 feet, he surpassed the record of a French diver who lost his life in such an attempt. At this point, the attorney hesitated, then began to descend once more. Somewhere below 550 feet, the man established a world record; but he lost his life in the depths.

Why did he fail to return to the surface? Could he have lost his sense of direction in the blackness of the deep water? The hypothesis of his team of assistants was that he succumbed to what the French free-diving fraternity calls the *rapture of the depths*. This is a kind of intoxication produced by the pressure and blackness of the deep water which lures its unfortunate victims beyond the point of safe return.

We, too, may find ourselves falling into this "rapture of the depths" by sinking into the darkness (negativity) of any experience and losing our sense of balance and direction. When anyone thinks too much about a problem, or remains too long in an attitude of negative thinking or emotions, there seems to be a magnetic pull that draws the person deeper into it. An alcoholic can have this type of experience, as can those who suffer an illness, lose a job, or go through a traumatic severance of a relationship.

Yet, regardless of how "bad" a situation may seem to be, no matter how long the circumstances may have continued, there is always help. It takes a lot of courage to face a dark situation, and even more self-control and discipline to draw attention from the negative experience and place it squarely on God, the universal power which is far greater than we. This is the time of letting go through the exclamation of, "I've had it! Enough! Life certainly must have more to offer!" And it does.

There is a God-self within each person that knows we can never be separated from our good. There is also a part of us that doesn't remember this Truth, and must, therefore, be reeducated. Every time we remember that we are made in the image and likeness of God, we rise higher in consciousness. The great struggle isn't with the world, but with self. We may be lured away from God thinking by appearances in the outer world, but the greater lure is our indwelling Christ presence. The adjustment takes place in our minds. Decide what you want, take command of yourself, and go get it! Simple words? Yes. Hard to accomplish? Yes! But possible!

What happens when you start working with the divine idea of the Rainbow Connection, realizing that God's promises are real and workable?

You gain . . .

a new sense of inner worth,

a wholesome self-respect,

the ability to successfully overcome all problems and handle all cacti gently, and with ease,

the ability to work successfully with others,

an overcoming of mental hang-ups,

a stabilizing of your emotional nature,
the power to overcome fear, stress, anxiety, and depression,
a greater understanding of yourself and other persons,
ideas! ideas! ideas!

If you purchased an item in a department store and, upon arriving home, found that it was unsuitable for you, what would you do? You would simply take the item back to the store and exchange it for something that was more suitable. How about unhappiness? Financial lack? Poor relationships? Can you exchange these "items" for joy, prosperity, and congeniality? Sure you can!

On a clear evening in the country, or atop a mountain, or in your own backyard, as you thoughtfully gaze at the luminous shining lamps of the universe scattered like seeds of light in the vast garden of space, think upon the immense reaches of the cosmos that are seemingly vacant and devoid of life. Yet, stretching into distances so tremendous that it boggles the mind to comprehend, stretching even beyond the elastic bands of your imagination, is the endless area which men call "space."

Our wondrous universe is an immortal tapestry upon which the Creator has woven bright stars and galaxies, great suns and enormous solar systems. The universe is the shuttle of cosmic magnetism, whose invisible ribbons of radiant energy connect all of the multifaceted parts of life into one harmonious whole. You are an important part of this whole, small though you seem. Remember that you are fearfully and wonderfully made. From its heart center, life pulses a constant flow of energy to sustain the consciousness, health, and harmony of your physical form.

People become aware of you and notice you as a definite and distinctive individual. Through sincere efforts, you have made those in your world conscious of the physical you they see. Through your words and actions, you have indicated that your mental self, as well as your physical self, is also distinctively individual. You are to be a source, not an interpreter or amplifier of what others may offer. You are you.

You can develop the ability to receive greater insight into yourself and into how you get where you are and how to go where you need to go. A greatly appreciated businessman once said, "When nothing seems to help, I go and watch a stonecutter hammering away at his rock. Perhaps he makes a hundred strokes without as much as a crack showing in the rock. Yet, as the hundred and first blow falls, the rock will split in half, and I know that it was not that particular blow that did it, but all the ones that had gone before."

At this moment, you are immersed in an infinite ocean of life. The power of divine love constantly permeates the world in which you live, move, and have your being. The moment you recognize its existence, the power and wisdom of this infinite energy become potent and active in your life. When this activity occurs, you experience an immediate and marvelous feeling of inner security, and discover the serenity and calm peace that flood your soul and keep you ever master over all situations.

One More Move

On a transcontinental flight, two young men were engrossed in a mind-stretching game of chess. They seemed to be at a stalemate when a fellow traveler, an older gentleman who had become intrigued by the game, moved into the adjoining seat alongside the activity. As one of the contestants was about to concede the game, the man touched his arm gently and said, "Wait! Look carefully at the board. There is one more move you can make!" The youth gestured for the man to take his place at the board and watched intently as the man made one deft move that changed the perspective of the game. After executing a few quick maneuvers, the game was won! As the younger men stared at each other in amazement, the man smiled and told them that when playing chess, one more move may not always be possible. However, in the game of life, when one's best efforts seemed to have failed, there was always one more move: letting go, and asking divine wisdom to solve the situation.

Several years later, the young player whose place had been taken in the chess game was called into the armed services and related a war experience upon his return home. Cut off from his company in a strange land, alone at night in a cold and damp foxhole, and with enemy patrols drawing closer, his life seemed dark, lost, and hopeless. Suddenly, he remembered the chess game and the man's statement that there is always one more move. He breathed a deep sigh and began to pray, asking God to take over in this desperate situation. He prayed with an authority that astonished himself. The tables turned! Under the cover of darkness, he surprised the enemy patrol, which wasn't as large as he first thought, causing them to lay down their guns and become his prisoners. His one move of allowing God to take charge turned a seemingly impossible situation into a life-saving occurrence, including his own!

In Psalms, chapter 55, verse 22, Scripture gives us a promise of encouragement: *Cast your burden on the Lord and he will sustain you* .... The action described in this promise works beautifully when human efforts have been exhausted. This one more move—letting God take control—changes what seems to be inevitable defeat into certain victory.

* Daniel, in the midst of a den of hungry lions, used his one more move. He remained unshakable in his faith that God would close the lions' mouths!

* David went forth to meet Goliath equipped with a stave, a sling, and his shepherd's pouch into which he put five smooth stones. He waited for the precise moment for his next move, then hurled the stone with deadly accu-

racy and saved the city of Keilah from the Philistines. And he used only one stone!

* Joseph, the Israelite lad from Canaan, although sold into slavery, had one more move and became the most powerful man at the court of the Egyptian Pharoah. He transformed his brother's treachery into forgiving love.
* Ruth exercised one more move by exhibiting loyalty to her mother-in-law and eventually became the great-grandmother of David, Israel's most illustrious king.
* Jesus, instead of conceding defeat, became the Way-Shower by proving that negative conditions can be resolved beyond expectation when we realize our true heritage as God's beloved children.

Sometimes negative conditions may seem to have multiplied to such a degree that we wonder if things can be righted. The temptation to slide into thinking that the only course of action available is to resign ourselves to the adversity and bear it submissively is a one-way roller coaster to defeat. Despair no longer. There is one more move!

The master Jesus promised that we can do all things when we abide in Him and His words abide in us. Listen! *"Do not fear, only believe."* (Mark 5:36) And how much assurance is given in the statement: *". . . lo, I am with you always."* (Matt. 28:20) Or, *". . . If you ask anything in my name, I will do it."* (John 14:14) Here, in these words of Truth, is our guarantee that one more move toward Spirit never fails.

You might remark, "One of these days, when thus and such has happened, I will make my Truth demonstration of a solution to this seemingly insoluble problem." Well, what is wrong with right now! Faith is like a muscle. It requires exercise to be strong and used most effectively. God's time is now! So is yours! Perhaps that one more move requires courage and effort of will to rise above threatening appearances. But you can do it. You can change circumstances in your life for the better. Affirm to yourself: *Today I make one more move. Regardless of appearances, I hold to the Truth that God's eternal love is active in my life. I cultivate spiritual reliance on God's universal laws. I invite the Christ Spirit to infill my mind and heart, completely and unconditionally. I release fear, doubt, and*

*anxiety. I am serene and strengthened, joy-
ous and expectant of my inflowing good.
Thank You, God.*

I have made one more move when courage
seemed at its lowest ebb and hope was so elevated a state of mind that it wasn't in my
vocabulary at the time. But the call com-
pelled the answer! A marvelous Truth about
making one more move toward divine Principle is that God, in His infinite love for
humanity, extends the invitation to, "Come
unto me." As we move into this uplifting flow
of love, we become like the prodigal son who
said: *"I will arise and go to my father . . . .*
(Luke 15:18) Of course, you know the story's
happy ending of the joyous welcome the returning wanderer received from his father.
The father ran to meet him while he was still
far off, and bestowed expensive gifts upon his
son. Yes, the Spirit of truth is within you, and
its wisdom, love, and power eagerly await to
give you the kingdom.

The Perpetual Prayer of Divine Action

Frequently I hear folks comment that they
wish greatly to change their lives. One or
more conditions exist that could use the

transmuting energy of love in action. For some, prosperity demonstrations are desired. Another may seek healing of a persistent illness. Someone else may seek increased harmony in business and personal relationships. The desires are as vast and different as people!

Several years ago, I found what I believe to be the most potent, powerful, and dynamic prayer for achievement! However, I caution you, *don't use this prayer unless you definitely want results and are ready to handle the conditions of change!* I call this prayer the perpetual prayer of divine action, and it works! It consists of six simple words:

"Here I AM, Lord. Use me!"

This prayer gets you out of the small thoughts of self and says to the universe that you are ready to handle the bigger vision. In the Bible, young Samuel opened himself up to the guidance of Spirit by announcing: ... *"Speak, for thy servant hears."* (I Samuel 3:10) Samuel listened, and went on to become one of the greatest, if not the greatest, judges in Israel.

Naturally, you desire to become the greatest you possible. And you are fully and wonderfully equipped with all the necessary ingredients for becoming an effective child of God, trailing clouds of glory! Use the prayer of openness and receptivity. If you seek to be a productive channel of expression for Spirit, if you are looking for true direction, if you wish to do what you can to create peace on Earth and good will for humanity's ongoing, I offer you this special prayer with all my love.

"Here I AM, Lord. Use me!"

A consciousness developed through holding an attitude of Truth and loving service removes you far from the lure of any depths. It develops an ability and power to hold all cacti in an open palm, to observe the message or learn the lesson, and then to gently place it aside. One more move may be all that's required for leaving behind all shackles (concepts) that bind you to any limitations, freeing you to go to the loving Father (illumined thought consciousness) so that you, too, may do all things that He did, and greater things, as is promised.

Maltie D. Babcock has said: *Our business in life is not to get ahead of other people, but to get ahead of ourselves. To break our own record, to outstrip our yesterdays by todays, to bear our trials more beautifully than we ever dreamed we could, to whip the tempter inside and out as we never whipped him before, to give as we have never given, to do our work with more force and a finer finish than ever, this is the true idea, to get ahead of ourselves. To beat someone else in a game, or to be beaten, may mean much or little.* To beat your own game means a great deal. *Whether we win or not, we are playing better than we ever did before, and that's the point after all—to play a better game of life.* (Taken from "A Treasury of the Art of Living" by Rabbi Sidney Greenberg.)

Rainbow Meditation

Oh, blessed child of Truth!

Can you now see; can you now know, that you are holiness as well as life, for life is holy?

The light in you radiates eternally. The world in which you live and work and play is sanctified because of your holy essence.

All living things bring you gifts, offering their treasures in gratitude and gladness for your beingness.

Flowers waft their delicate perfumes around you. Infuse their fragrance in your totality.

The waves of the great sea roll at your feet. Absorb their healing energy.

Trees spread their arms to shield you from heat and rain, and lay their leaves along your path so that you may tread with footsteps soft. Rest in their hospitality.

The wind whispers affirmations of the elements around your holy head. Hear now the music of the spheres.

The sun reverences the solar fire blazing from the brilliance of your soul. Attune one to one.

Yea, the universe beholds your light. All living things are still before you, for they recognize who walks as constant companion with you. Your light is your inner reality that cannot be hidden—the reality that is universally true.

All of life is reflected through you. Accept this reverence. It is due to creativity, which walks with you, transforming in its gentle love-light all life into its image and likeness and purity.

Walk with God in perfect holiness.

Humanity—The Planetary Lightbearer!

It must ever be borne in mind that the great theme of light underlies our entire planetary purpose.—Alice Bailey

𝓙n some unusual manner, from the human aspect, that which concerns the development of humankind has been expressed all through the ages in various terms of illumination and knowledge, of sight and of the entrance of light, leading to increasing revelations on all levels of awareness. Through the activity of the spiritual light of the soul, human vision expands and the plan of divine purpose is released into our thinking, feeling, and manifestation.

At this point in human history, we stand on the brink of a tremendous spiritual potency and unlimited opportunity for all upon the path of discipleship. What is meant by discipleship? The Merriam-Webster Dictionary describes a *disciple* as *a pupil or follower who helps spread his master's teachings.* We are all disciples of God, or Truth, seeking in our individual ways to share what we know with others, extending helping hands to fellow travelers along the way even as we have received from those who have gone before us.

At times, we become so involved in the life experiences of day-to-day living that we may forget to consciously apply the Truth we know. We forget that we are cosmic beings! We forget that we are definitely capable of meeting all situations and doing something constructive about them! We seem to forget that *the Christ presence is with us at all times, eager to respond to our call.*

After the crucifixion of Jesus, the disciples forgot occasionally the most important teaching He gave them: "... *lo, I am with you always ... !*" (Matt. 28:20) They forgot His teaching that they were sons of the Most High—one with God—and that they had the Christ within which would help them in any circumstance.

After Jesus was no longer with the disciples in physical form, they became disturbed.

One of the first thoughts to enter their minds was, "We must get busy making a living." It was a nice dream, but it didn't work!

Peter said, "I will go fishing."

The others said, "We will go with you." Scripture tells the story thusly: (John 21:1-14)

After this Jesus revealed himself again to the disciples by the Sea of Tiberias; and he revealed himself in this way. Simon Peter, Thomas called the Twin, Nathanael of Cana in Galilee, the sons of Zebedee, and two others of his disciples were together. Simon Peter said to them, "I am going fishing." They said to him, "We will go with you." They went out and got into the boat; but that night they caught nothing.

Just as day was breaking, Jesus stood on the beach; yet the disciples did not know that it was Jesus. Jesus said to them, "Children, have you any fish?" They answered him, "No."

He said to them, "Cast the net on the right side of the boat, and you will find some."

So they cast it, and now they were not able to haul it in, for the quantity of fish.

That disciple whom Jesus loved said to Peter, "It is the Lord!" When Simon Peter heard that it was the Lord, he put on his clothes, for he was stripped for work, and sprang into the sea. But the other disciples came in the boat, dragging the net full of fish, for they were not far from the land, but about a hundred yards off.

When they got out on land, they saw a charcoal fire there, with fish lying on it, and bread. Jesus said to them, "Bring some of the fish that you have just caught." So Simon Peter went aboard and hauled the net ashore, full of large fish, a hundred and fifty-three of them; and although there were so many, the net was not torn. Jesus said to them, "Come and have breakfast." Now none of the disciples dared ask him, "Who are you?" They knew it was the Lord. Jesus came and took the bread and gave it to them, and so with the fish. This was now the third time that Jesus was revealed to the disciples after he was raised from the dead.

Let's look at this story more closely. The disciples entered a boat and fished all night.

They labored and toiled without success and became tired and weary. When they returned the next morning, Jesus was standing on the shore. What is the inner meaning of this aspect of the story?

When we return to our inner being after a hard struggle of trying to solve our problems the human way, we find the Christ is always present, awaiting our recognition of Him.

Jesus asked the disciples if they had any fish. Upon hearing their negative reply, He instructed them to *"cast the net on the right side of the boat"* and they would find fish. In fact, the disciples, upon following the Master's instructions, found so many fish they couldn't pull them all aboard the boat.

Like all Bible texts, a great lesson may be obtained by placing ourselves in the identities of the main characters in this incidence. The Lord, or Jesus, represents the Christ, or I AM, within us. Peter and the disciples represent the spiritual faculties of our being. Notice that *when your disciples (twelve inner faculties) are not directed by you, they may cause problems.*

The disciples did not recognize the Master because Peter (representing faith) was nearly naked. But the moment he clothed himself, he recognized the Christ. John (representing love) was the first to recognize Jesus which indicates that love recognizes the Christ before faith does.

The sea represents the mental realm in which we exist and the fish are multitudinous divine ideas. Our minds are the net which catches the fishes (ideas!), and these thoughts are the basis of all external experiences and conditions.

The right side of the boat represents the side on which we realize the eternal Truth which states that inexhaustible resources are ever present and can be made manifest by those who exercise faith in the proper direction.

Jesus' instruction was to *"cast the net on the right side."* So, with fish representing ideas, casting the net on the right side says to us the importance of thinking positive and true thoughts.

What a marvelous rainbow story, filled with promise! William James said: *The greatest discovery of this generation is that human beings can alter their lives by changing their mental attitude.* Repeatedly through various Truth studies the same instruction presents itself. You may not always control the conditions that come into your life, or how other people act, but you can determine how you will act or react to all people, places, and situations. As your thoughts become increasingly positive and aligned with universal law, your consciousness is elevated; and as your individual consciousness is elevated, you play an important part in raising the consciousness of the entire human race.

You are important! Everything you say, think, feel, and do is important! You are a planetary citizen, a wonderful part of a magnificent whole. Astronaut Edgar Mitchell said: *No man I know of has gone to the moon and come back that has not been affected in some way that is very similar. It is what I prefer to call instant global consciousness. Each man comes back with a feeling that he is no longer only an American citizen; he is a planetary citizen. He doesn't like the way things are and he wants to improve it. It is a universal feeling among the astronauts.*

Isn't it tremendous that people are waking up now to this awareness and to this responsibility! You, too, can have an experience similar to the astronauts' by viewing within your mind's eye and heart the world as a precious whole, and seeing it as a planetary home.

Realities glimpsed from afar are seen as ideals. When viewed from closer range, they are the practical necessities of the time. Brotherhood-sisterhood and human unification are like that. Human events are swiftly carrying us toward their realization with tremendous speed in this important time in cosmic history. It is the hour when the clarion call goes forth to all to be filled with light, to be of good cheer, and to exercise good will. It is the hour when opening one's eyes to immediate problems or situations is a necessity. No longer do we grope in ignorance.

Jesus gave us an immense lesson in spirituality when He told His disciples to come and dine. Upon receiving the guidance of Spirit, you must respond and follow that guidance in order to receive the good you are seeking. *You* are the one who must take action. Jesus speaks of a positive consciousness: *"For to every one who has will more be given, and he will have abundance; but from him who has not, even what he has will be taken away."* (Matthew 25:29) Does this sound unfair? Do you understand what this

Scripture means?

"*. . . to every one who has will more be given*" denotes a positive consciousness that is like a mighty magnet, drawing to it in accord with the outgoing energy vibrations. Whereas, a negative consciousness repels the good that God has for each of us.

We become the perfect children of God when we abide in the consciousness of being perfect children of God—when we are casting our nets on the right side.

Jesus said: "*But seek first his kingdom and his righteousness, and all these things shall be yours as well.*" (Matthew 6:33) Read this Scripture and replace the word *kingdom* with the word *consciousness,* and note what happens! Seek the consciousness of God and make right use of the ideas He gives, then all other things shall be added. That's a promise I can believe in!

The Energy of Light

The subjective purpose of manifestation has been said to be the development and relating of mind and heart. Two great spiritual teachers stand head and shoulders above all others in the archives of history as planetary lightbearers. The Buddha is universally regarded as the embodiment of light. His precepts and teachings provided a mighty tool enabling man to come to terms with his mind, to walk the "middle path," finding the way between pairs of opposites through the practice of detachment and dispassion. The eventually achieved result was illumination and wisdom.

We know the other, and greatest teacher, as Jesus Christ, truly the embodiment of love. The new commandment He brought to mankind transcended in one profound injunction all systems of life and ethics based on the negative Thou-shalt-nots. He said: *"This is my commandment, that you love one another as I have loved you. Greater love has no man than this, that a man lay down his life for his friends .... This I command you, to love one another."* (John 15:12-17)

Life is paradoxical. An Eastern saying states that, "The mind is the slayer of the real." We see the Truth in this quote when we observe how the narrow intellectualism and so-called logic of the human mind can divest life of its real and true meaning. How many times have you "logicized" a good idea out of existence! Only when the human mind comes under the influence of love is it definitely enlightened and becomes the medium of revelation.

By the same token, it can be said that love is blind if the balancing power of mind and the light which gives wisdom and understanding are absent from the thinking process. Mind is the feature that distinguishes humanity from other evolutions. The spark of intelligence lifted man above the animal kingdom, allowing him the joy of walking in the light of his soul. Through the light, that which is in darkness becomes totally apparent. All chaos and misery stand revealed, awaiting the transmuting energy of love. We see the sorrows of the world in transition as the Holy Spirit whispers of redemptive grace and love. Do we have the ability to face the revelation of the light and progress forward, contributing our utmost and sure of the ultimate triumph of Good? I think so!

The Shaft of Light

The thought of more light governs all the inchoate yearnings of the human spirit. It was this realization that prompted Dag Hammerskjöld's brilliantly conceived epitome of

such yearnings in the symbol he set before
the men of all nations in the Meditation
Room in the United Nations buildings in New
York:

*... there are simple things which speak
to us all with the same language. We
have sought such things and we believe
that we have found them in the shaft of
light striking the shining surface of solid
rock.*

*So, in the middle of the room we see a
symbol of how, daily, the light of the
skies gives life to the earth on which we
stand, a symbol to many of us of how the
light of the spirit gives life to matter.*

*... the shaft of light strikes the stone
in a room of utter simplicity. There are no
other symbols, there is nothing to dis-
tract our attention or to break in on the
stillness within ourselves ....*

*We want to bring back the stillness
which we have lost in our streets and in
our conference rooms, and to bring it
back in a setting in which no noise would
impinge upon our imagination. In that
setting we want to bring back our
thoughts to elementary facts, the facts
we are always facing, life struck by light*

while resting on the ground. Dag Hammarskjöld.

Later, one of Dag Hammarskjöld's close friends, in a conversation about the Meditation Room, said, "There was nothing in that room chosen to represent a religion, yet it seemed to have the power to convey to all men of all religions, or of none, the attitude that has to precede human understanding of any quality—a sense of humility and of quietude. For many of us, the rock and the light express something of the range within which the human spirit could unfold into infinity or be locked into solidness like stone."

Human beings are able to think for themselves, but until they do so intelligently and become willing to understand the great principles upon which our universe rests, they cannot respond to the motivating force and driving power of God's divine plan for all of humanity. Oh, humans, open your eyes! Think! God can give you the wisdom to meet and handle every situation. The wisdom of God is at work in you. The wisdom of God is at work in every situation. Every problem has a solution. If some aspect of life seems difficult, if a ready answer doesn't seem to appear, affirm divine wisdom: *I meet all things with strength, courage, and confidence, for God gives me the wisdom to meet and handle every situation.*

Remember that the eternal spirit of love is light. Rise above every concern for the future even though it may seem to be disturbed and obscure. Step forward into a fuller sphere of existence and of reality. Recognize God's infinite power and yield to it that you may enter the temple of light.

The Union of Power and Love

The great poet, Robert Browning, published a poem called "Reverie" in which he avowed his faith that here or hereafter, the union of power and love would be accomplished.

I have faith such end shall be:
From the first, Power was—I knew.
Life has made clear to me
That, strive but for closer view,
Love were as plain to see.

Probably never before in recorded history have so many minds been engaged in a consciousness of transcendent issues involved in success or failure in finding a practical solution. When the first atomic bomb destroyed a city, destroyed also were the complacent illusions of those who denied religion and claimed that science is a panacea for all the ills of mankind and an absolute guarantee of the arrival of an earthly paradise.

No political or other system of defense against hideous weapons of destruction can permanently secure immunity from their use by persons who are indifferent to their fatal and terrible consequences. Now is the time when the beloved Master's commandment to love one another must express itself in love of humanity. It is love toward your neighbor that brings peace within your heart, which establishes and furthers peace on Earth.

Love is the great cohesive force of our universe, for where there is love, no separation exists. It is a mighty force of transmutation which transforms the person—body, mind, and soul—into a spiritual being. God's divine plan for mankind cannot fulfill itself. We cannot complete the evolutionary cycle of returning to the Source without the operation of the love principle. A great teacher said, "Love heals the wounds caused by ignorance and makes all of creation whole in all its aspects. The full miracle of love is beyond comprehension, but we here and you, our brethren of

Earth, can come to understand more and more about it by experiencing the many ways in which it works and its incredible results."

What is the measure of one's love for Truth? *"Greater love has no man,"* than to lay down the human self through losing the ego personality identity by consciously becoming a part of the whole. Those who would serve as planetary lightbearers have three action steps which can be accomplished now!

1. Cultivate the light of wisdom, and establish a loving relationship with God's will and purpose, which enables all things to be seen in right perspective and proportion.

2. Unfold the light of understanding within yourself, for it is the light that links humanity to the heart and love of God and to the compassion of the universe.

3. Increase your light of knowledge, for attunement with knowledge coupled with capacity to make use of it reflects as wisdom shining from within you. The light of knowledge relates you to the mind of God.

As these three aspects of love light unfold within yourself, increased light radiates from you to the livingness of all things, and thereby you serve. How do you physically dissipate darkness? You turn on a light! Darkness is only a void with no existence. Problems, troubles, and pain are voids in our thinking capacity—empty potential areas, waiting for creation through loving, spiritual thoughts to fill them. When you recreate yourself, bit by bit, by filling mental voids, by dissipating ignorance, by increasing knowledge and understanding, by turning on enlightenment of Truth in your consciousness, the glory of the Creator is released and it becomes apparent that *the Lord is in His holy temple.*

See how silently the golden light lifts
    above the horizon at dawn.

Hear the hush of the sacred hour that
    comes as a new day is born.

Feel the serenity of a period, preciously
    spent, when mind and body are quiescent, receptive to God's blessings.

Immerse yourself in the radiance of the
    Holy Spirit.

For a time, words cease. Thoughts are
    stilled. Feelings are calmed.

Prayers are gentled. Inharmony disappears. Resentments are resolved.

Dislikes are transmuted into love.

The Lord is in His holy temple.

Quietly and easily the glory of your inner light ascends above the horizon of personal struggle and reveals the divine Presence. It is your ever-present help, your all-sufficiency for every need. Your soul is lifted in pure adoration. Personal consciousness is elevated to touch the great Divine Mind and you are joyously awakened to your inner power!

By now, you realize that all the individual points of God's man-idea are equal reflections of the absolute whole—like the facets of a brilliant diamond, pointing away from each other, and from the center in which they have their being. Each may be unaware of the existence of any but itself. However, someone who is detached and has a greater view observes the entire stone and can see all the individual facets as equal parts of the whole. The faculty that brings forth this great knowledge and understanding is love, God's principle of fulfillment in all creation.

The Universal Law of Love in Action

An invisible force governs the winds, the tides, the seasons, the birthing of spring flowers and immense growth of forests, the mating of the species, the glorious sunlight, and the myriad twinkling stars. A vast, understanding beneficence embraces all creation. An infinite compassion exists for all sorrows. A universal celebration heralds all joy. God, the Fountainhead, is no capricious being. In His wondrous creation all life is equal, from the smallest to the greatest. For permeating everything that is, is a portion of His own most perfect existence, absolute love. He can do no less than love all his handiwork, for love, to be perfect, must contain the elements of compassion and forbearance.

Pure love and the power and capacity to love points to the existence of things to be loved. This is a secret of creation.

Gain wisdom so that you do not love unwisely and lose your sense of proportion. Be master over your emotions so that the balance of good is maintained. Sometimes, in emotional eagerness to love, we may rob a fellow traveler of an important life-lesson and thereby delay his onward progress. Love wisely. One of the greatest ways to achieve a higher expression of love is through the highways and byways of experiencing love toward all other people and forms of life. One of the most important things in the world is to understand love and use it properly. If we can but do this, we would be transformed and all of life would be pure joy.

In order to fulfill Jesus' commandment to love, and to express love as He did, we must lift our vision and identify ourselves as more than mere human beings. Now is the time to realize that we are God-creations. We are citizens of a universe. We are planetary light-bearers! Your presence can become a benediction to all who come in contact with you. Every place you stand is holy ground because you are there! If good is present where you are, it is because you have brought it there. It is a manifestation of your consciousness! Is it so hard to believe the truth about yourself? There is much work to be done. We all have our assignments.

Rainbow Meditation

*I am a human being, sharing life with all in
    my world.
Countless other lives interweave with mine,
    human and non-human,
Creating a wholeness called planet Earth.
My existence resides in this wholeness,
    making me
A planetary citizen.
I am one with the forces of growth and
    unfoldment.
Consciousness, operating through imagina-
    tion, enables me
To direct these forces with knowledge,
    wisdom, and skill.
I explore possibilities of what can be, and
    I create.
Because I have this creative consciousness,
Because I am a unique part of humanity, and
Because you are a unique part of humanity,
We cocreate.
Together, we build a community of love.*

We dream and learn and know and change.
We serve as planetary lightbearers and
Help fulfill the destiny of life upon this world.
No limits are placed on our capacity to create
Or on our capacity to be of loving service to
others;
For loving service is the key to our human
identity
And our fulfillment as the human race.

Behold! We are made perfect with our feet
planted firmly on Earth
And our arms outstretched in attitudes of
service and blessing.
The star of light shines like a jewel from our
heart centers
Wherein lies the seed atom of the Christ
Spirit,
The jewel within the lotus.

Activities for a Modern Disciple

*W*here are You, God within?

Have you ever asked yourself that question? I have! In fact, many times I've felt like standing on tiptoe, taking the biggest, deepest breath I can hold, and shouting, "Come out, come out, wherever You are!"

How do you go about finding something you've misplaced? Remember playing hide-and-seek as a child? It's rather like that. God within, I know You're within somewhere—in my bones and joints, nerves and muscles, veins and arteries, and perhaps my heart!

I've seen God within in other persons as a twinkle in the eye, a kind word, an unexpected smile, a musician's melody. The great classics in word and music refer to this special something. Jesus referred to the Presence within, so I'm positive there *is* God within.

Jesus' life was a constant example of what

can be accomplished when someone accepts and acknowledges the presence of God within. Jesus said, in effect, "Anything I can do, you can do better!" And Jesus fed five thousand! Jesus told parables to those who followed Him which affected the listener at his particular level of consciousness. Jesus healed the sick and raised the dead. Since He told us we can do what He did, and more, why don't we believe it and do it! Do you suppose Jesus was talking about some "you" other than yourself? No! It is the God within each person that He was talking about. We *can* do it!

Come Out, Come Out, Wherever You Are!

Sometimes, taking a lighter look at an idea or situation helps me to understand it better and easier. I admit, God within is not always easy to contact in our present states of consciousness. But it can be done! Jesus' every cell was in harmony and tuned into the universal source of God's energy and love. He could tap into this unlimited universal source of all abundance because He knew He was a part of the source and the source was part of Him! We need to know this, too.

A question that often occupies my mind is this: Since we are individual expressions of God, since the same Spirit abides in us that performed the miracles through Jesus, since the kingdom of heaven is within, since we come into earth-life trailing clouds of glory, then why are we not manifesting this power through our daily works?

The Christ within you says: "... *he who believes in me will also do the works that I do; and greater works than these will he do, because I go to the Father. Whatever you ask in my name, I will do it, that the Father may be glorified in the Son; if you ask anything in my name, I will do it.*" (John 14:12-14) Are we not doing these works because we don't understand what is meant, don't accept the Truth that is given, don't realize that we do have this power within, and don't take action? Probably so!

Is it so difficult to believe, especially as Truth students, that we arrived on this planet fully equipped with everything required to be happy and successful? This statement is worthy of repeating to ourselves until we are absolutely convinced of its reality.

In the beginning, God took the real you—

your consciousness, or soul—and gave it a body and a mind, *His Mind.* Then He gave you free will, the freedom to think for yourself and make decisions. Jesus wouldn't say *"Be ye perfect,"* if it weren't possible for you to do so. The Master Way-Shower knew we were created with full potential, with all power and authority. He knew such mightiness couldn't be drawn out if it weren't already within. This process is called involution and evolution.

Involution is God's implanting His image-likeness in us. *Evolution* is the gradual and orderly coming forth of God through us. There is a spiritual law of perfection working in and through us, emerging under the law of evolution. Oh, that we become as children to see the wondrous Truth before us.

God is ever-present consciousness, aware of itself as life, wholeness, order, and peace. Consciousness always outpictures itself, appearing as form or body. However, your reality is not only your body but the state of consciousness which produced your body. What you see is the form, the temple, wherein dwells the Christ Spirit. The Christ within is your resurrecting power. Your resurrection can occur as naturally as apples come forth on an apple tree in the spring. Expression is an inside job!

We shared earlier some thoughts about a disciple—a pupil or follower who helps spread his master's teachings. Let's look at some important tools we have available to assist ourselves, as well as others, in the activity of resurrection.

Spiritual "I" Glasses

Scripture tells us: ... *Eye hath not seen, nor ear heard, neither have entered into the heart of man, the things which God hath prepared for them that love him.* (I Cor. 2:9 A.V.) For most persons, regular eye examinations have been an important means of caring for the physical eyes. Our eyes perform a marvelous function and we appreciate the wonder of their creation. An even more meaningful examination is that of inspecting the inner "I." It is through our awareness of this inner "I" that we find the power and the secret spiritual growth taught by Jesus. He said: ... *"I am the way, and the truth, and the life."* (John 14:6) The great I AM is the creative principle of the universe, and as we attune our minds with this creative principle, we discover the God consciousness we so diligently seek. A lifetime, perhaps many lifetimes, unfold as we learn the nature of our inner "I." An effective affirmation for increasing awareness of the inner "I" states:

I AM a spiritual being, living in a spiritual universe governed by spiritual laws; and as a spiritual being, I AM having a human experience as I journey in a physical world created through the power of my thoughts.

Become more familiar with the mighty I AM of you. If the difficulties and varied experiences of life would be more fully understood, enter through humility and simplicity into the inner sanctuary of the Christ. Within you is archived the history of creation. Pursuit of spiritual activities leads you ever onward and upward toward liberation from the bonds of flesh and into divine illumination. The glorious Christ Spirit within you, the activity of the eternal I AM will crown you, not with thorns, but with the luminous crown of God-illumination.

As you recognize the power of thought to create your world, also examine your feelings and words, for they mold and fashion the shape of this world. After all, the purpose of any eye ("I") exam is to ascertain that you see as clearly as possible!

Attributes of a Disciple of Truth

Sincere and true disciples of Truth are those who are conscious builders in the now for the future of humanity. They use their time wisely in the growing of their souls so they may more effectively serve their own divine plans and God's plan for mankind. They live for all that is beauty, goodness, and Truth by building bridges between the lower and higher minds, between lower and higher degrees of consciousness. Their ultimate goals are the great services that they can give to humanity through their own life conditions.

1. They live lives of *harmlessness* which places them in the vibration of the law of love. Harmlessness is love in action and evokes a spiritual response in other persons. All of nature is supportive of the harmless one.

2. They live lives of loving understanding which synthesizes their comprehension with those with whom they

come in contact, and they are better able to communicate with each person.

3. They make right use of all the energies pouring through all aspects of their being. Fear cannot penetrate their consciousness, for all their actions are honest and righteous.

4. They work from a higher mental plane and exercise right human relationships, clear thinking, and good will.

5. They are "single-eyed" in Christ attunement and cannot be sidetracked by money, position, reputation, fear, flattery, or bribery.

6. They joyfully and lovingly uphold all personal, family, and national duties and responsibilities because they care.

7. They live in humility, fulfilling the Scripture: *"Blessed are the meek, for they shall inherit the earth."*

8. Their creative originality is exhibited in all that they do, for their work lives with the powers of inspiration and intuition.

9. They make no boisterous claims.

Their work speaks for their reality. That which is entrusted to them in secret is held as a sacred trust within their hearts.

10. Their teachings are based upon the great truths presented through the ages and the chain of revelations of Jesus Christ and other lightbearers.

Code of Conduct for a New Age Disciple

You do not know when life may call you into a more meaningful position, so be prepared to move with the flow of Spirit when such a summons comes. To a tape recorder the only time is now! As the tape flows by the recording head, the condition of the tape is changed in the instantaneous now which is the split-second of its passing.

So it is with our minds. Now is where we are. Now is the only moment. We cannot experience anything except in the now. Oh, yes, our tape recorder has a re-wind button which enables us to review what has gone before. But we are unable to change what has already been recorded except in how we think about it. The fast forward button rapidly moves us forward to a portion of the tape to which we have not yet listened, but the future we are monitoring is experienced because it has become the now! Memories are brought into the now to be experienced. It seems immensely important to make the now of life as worthwhile and effective as possible. How can this be done?

1. Be conscious that you aspire to the full expression of God, and devote your service and being to that end.

2. Learn the lesson of harmlessness and neither by word nor thought nor feeling inflict negativity on any part of life. Understand that physical violence is a lesser part of the error of harmful expression.

3. Stir not a fellow traveler's sea of emotion, thoughtlessly or deliberately. Know that the storm in which you may place his soul will ultimately flow upon the shore of your own lifestream. Strive to bring tranquillity to life, and be the one who, as the Psalmist says, pours oil on troubled waters.

4. Disassociate yourself from personal delusion. Love the harmony of the universe more than the little self.

Refuse the snare of self-righteousness.

5. Walk gently through the universe with an understanding that your body is a temple in which dwells the Holy Spirit that brings peace and illumination to all life. Be respectful of the body temple, keeping it in a manner that befits the Spirit of Truth. Respect and honor with dignity all other temples, knowing that at times within what seems a crude exterior burns a great light.

6. Absorb the abundant and beautiful gifts of nature with a heart overflowing with gratitude. Take care not to despoil that which God has created.

7. Be flexible in thought so you are never endangered by crystallization. The breaking up process can be painful indeed. There is always another idea one hasn't received; there is always another avenue of thought one hasn't traveled. Keep the door of the mind open in welcome for new awareness.

8. Speak, when prompted by the Voice from within. Otherwise, remain

peacefully silent. Keep your own counsel.

9. Let your living of the laws of life speak for your integrity. A clanging gong is unnecessary to proclaim your aspiration to Godliness. Your heart can sing a song of gratitude that the Most High has given into your keeping.

10. Be alert to use your faculties and talents in such a manner that the Earth is a better place because you are here.

11. Claim nothing for yourself, neither powers nor principalities, any more than you would claim the air you breathe or the sun that touches your brow. Use all in your world freely, knowing that God is owner of all.

12. Let your watchwords be gentleness, strength, sincerity, and loving service. The servant of Truth, like the sun in the heavens, is eternally vigilant and constantly outpouring the essence of his reality.

An essential of life is to keep in touch with your divine heritage and to allow the magnificent presence of God within to find expression through you. The world is filled with beauty, joy, and power, even as it abounds with the presence of God. You have the opportunity and ability to share in all the treasures of our planetary home as you attune with your divine plan and open inwardly to God and outwardly toward mankind. Each time an opportunity comes your way that will allow you to express who and what you are, welcome that opportunity with open arms!

Remember that the word "spiritual" relates to attitudes, to relationships, to moving forward from one degree of consciousness to the next. It is related to the power to see the higher vision and explore the greater possibilities. It refers to every effect of the evolutionary process of life as it guides us onward from one range of sensitivity to another. It relates to expansions of consciousness and to all activity that leads toward some form of future development. As you grow in recognizing your own spiritual development and nature, you will more easily and quickly recognize the divinity in others and in all forms of life. As we begin to think of each other as divine, we will begin to act accordingly!

The highest Truth you now know presents but a part of the reality. Think not, my friend, to settle down eternally in the belief system of any one Truth. Instead, praise God from whom all blessings flow and give thanks to the universe.

May the joy of resurrection fill your heart, and may it be renewed daily.

May the presence of the beloved Master be felt in your innermost being, your home, and your activities.

May your heart be opened to the blessings from all the great teachers who have gone before, paving the way.

May you be aware of your linkage with the radiant life of God everywhere and, especially,

May you fulfill your destiny as a New Age disciple!

Rainbow Meditation

The Geat Invocation

*From the point of Light within the Mind
of God
Let light stream forth into the minds of
men.
Let Light descend on Earth.*

*From the point of Love within the Heart
of God
Let love stream forth into the hearts of
men.
May Christ return to earth.*

*From the center where the will of God is
known
Let purpose guide the little wills of men—
The purpose which the Masters know
and serve.*

*From the center which we call the race of
men
Let the Plan of Love and Light work out
And may it seal the door where evil
dwells.*

Let Light and Love and Power restore the Plan on Earth.

The above Invocation or prayer does not belong to any person or group but to all humanity. The beauty and the strength of this Invocation lie in its simplicity, and in its expression of certain central truths which all men, innately and normally, accept—the truth of the existence of a basic Intelligence to Whom we vaguely give the name of God; the truth that behind all outer seeming, the motivating power of the universe is Love; the truth that a great Individuality came to earth, called by Christians, the Christ, and embodied that love so that we could understand; the truth that both love and intelligence are effects of what is called the Will of God; and finally, the self-evident truth that only through humanity itself can the divine Plan work out.—Alice A. Bailey

Printed U.S.A.   163-F-6129-15M-7-83